Asparagus
The
Sparrowgrass
Cookbook

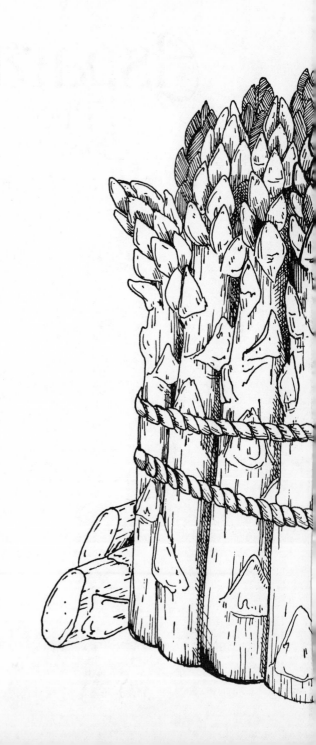

Asparagus
The Sparrowgrass Cookbook

By Autumn Stanley

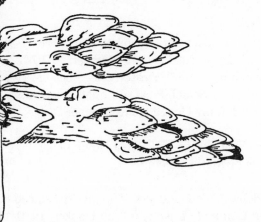

Pacific Search Press/cooking

International Standard Book Number: 0-914718-22-3
Library of Congress Catalog Card Number: 77-074273
Pacific Search Press, 715 Harrison Street, Seattle, WA 98109
© 1977 by Pacific Search Press. All rights reserved.
Manufactured in the United States of America

Cover and Page Design by Pamela Hoffman
Illustrations by Mari Eckstein

"Ranch House Green Goddess Soup" is reproduced from the book
Vegetarian Gourmet Cookery, © Alan Hooker, 1970, by
permission of the publisher, 101 Productions, San Francisco.

To Solveig and Humphrey,
whose asparagus started it all.

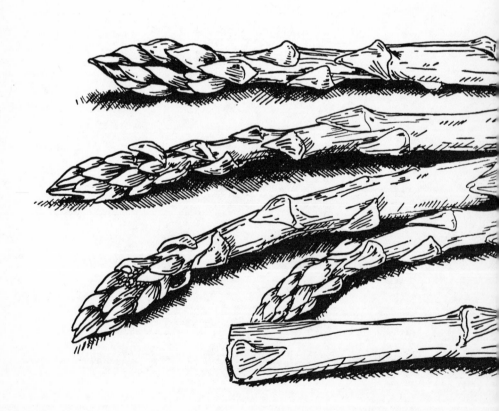

Contents

Introduction

Stalked in the wild since long before written records, cultivated by the Greeks, spread over much of the then-known world by the Romans, and apparently brought to the New World by both Dutch and English settlers, *Asparagus officinalis* and its close relatives have had a long and noble history. Emperors have doted on asparagus, gourmets have dated spring by it, Manet painted two pictures of it, and Proust was struck by its beautiful color. James Beard has said, "For my money, asparagus is one of the greatest gifts from the Old World to the New."

Until now, strangely enough, nobody has done a cookbook devoted to asparagus. Maybe this is because some people think there are only a few ways to serve asparagus: plain or with salt alone, with butter and salt, or with hollandaise sauce. If pressed, some may remember asparagus au gratin, asparagus vinaigrette, and cream of asparagus soup. But, as this book will show, there are more than a hundred ways to serve asparagus. There is even an asparagus dessert!

History

The lily we call asparagus is native to East Central Europe—especially southern Poland and Russia—to Greece, and to Asia Minor. It may even have grown in Egypt during the Memphite Dynasties. It grows wild in many other parts of the world today—where Euell Gibbons stalked it along California's irrigation canals, and on Asparagus Island in Cornwall, England—but these stands probably started from cultivation.

The Greeks were cultivating asparagus as early as 600 B.C. The Romans took it from the Greeks and introduced it into their homeland and throughout their European Empire—to the Gauls, the Germans, and the Britons. If we doubt this, we have only to look at the word for asparagus in all the modern European languages. The original Greek *asparagos* came from a Persian word meaning "sprout" or "shoot." The Latin was *asparagus,* like the modern English, though in sixteenth- and seventeenth-century English it was *sperage* or sometimes *sperach.* *Spaargus* displaced *sperage,* and then itself became corrupted to *sparrowgrass,* which was the polite form all during the eighteenth century. People who grow, market, or process asparagus still call it *grass.* The modern Italian is *sparagio,* the German *spargel,* the French *esperage,* and the Spanish *espárrago(s).*

Asparagus was obviously well known in classical times. Cato described its cultivation about 200 B.C. Pliny, about A.D. 75, complained about all the effort spent in the Ravenna district to grow asparagus so fat that three spears made a pound, when perfectly good wild asparagus was available for the picking. In the ruins of Pompeii was found a menu for a feast. The sixth dish of the *gustatio,* or appetizer course, was fat pullet with asparagus.

As the centuries passed, France and Holland both became noted for fine asparagus, and the Ravenna district of Italy kept the reputation Pliny had complained about. In London in 1667, Samuel Pepys bought 100 spears of "sparrowgrass," as it was called by then, for a shilling and sixpence.

By 1672, asparagus had already reached New England. And in March of 1773, President Blair of William and Mary College in Virginia was eating hothouse asparagus.

Asparagus was not only what anthropologists call a potherb (or vegetable), but a medicine. In fact, it was probably a medicine long before it was a food. Decoctions, wine extracts, syrups, and teas were made of the roots, sprouts, stems, and seeds. These liquids and pastes were drunk, plastered on the skin, or held in the mouth to cure (or help) everything from toothache and dropsy to jaundice, heart trouble, and kidney stones. A mixture of asparagus and oil was even supposed to prevent bee stings.

The second-century Greek physician Galen described asparagus as "heating, cleansing, and dessicative. It relieves inflammation of the stomach, relaxes the bowels, makes urine, and helps the weak. It removes obstruction of the liver and kidneys. . . ." Galen's teachings were law in the Western world for thirteen hundred years, and the strong tradition underlying those teachings dies hard. Claims for medicinal benefits of asparagus persisted well into the twentieth century in the minds of European peasants (and cookbook writers). Today, no one seriously claims any medicinal properties. We now generally understand that it is a good source of the vitamins A and C, and of the minerals potassium and phosphorus. It is also low in calories when not smothered in sauces.

The phallic shape of asparagus sprouts probably suggested one of the plant's second major uses—as an aphrodisiac. Pliny wrote about this idea, and Culpeper's herbal declared: "The decoction of the roots boiled in wine. . . being taken fasting several mornings together, stirreth

11

up bodily lust in man or woman, whatever some have written to the contrary."

When Louis XIV had asparagus in January, it came from the forcing beds of Versailles. Today, fresh asparagus is available in much of the world for far more of the year than it once was. The United States produces enormous amounts, primarily in California, Oregon, Utah, Kansas, Michigan, and New Jersey; some American growers airlift their *grass* to European markets.

In Europe, Germany and the Low Countries are also centers for asparagus. Gourmets there generally prefer the home-grown product, especially the delicate white asparagus that has never been allowed to see the sun. In the Black Forest of Germany stands a hotel called the Tettnang that has a separate menu (a Spargel Karte) just for its asparagus dishes—all *twenty-six* of them. France has several districts that pride themselves on their asparagus, the most famous of which is the Argenteuil. Argenteuil is not only a place, you see, but a variety of asparagus, developed in a research center established there about 1860, and undoubtedly improved over the years.

Growing Asparagus

Although it used to take years for asparagus to grow from seeds to its first harvest, you can now buy or order mature crowns from a nursery and wait only one to two years for your first harvest. Get sixty to seventy crowns for a family of four real asparagus lovers; about two dozen for an ordinary small family. Three good varieties are Mary Washington rust-resistant, U.C. 711, and California 500; if you like lighter-colored asparagus you might try Conover's Colossal or Mammoth White.

Since asparagus is faithful and forever, as Marjorie Blanchard puts it in *The Home Gardener's Cookbook,* locate your asparagus bed with care. The plants will need full sun, and room for their summer foliage (four to six feet tall and three feet wide), and they will need it for at least fifteen to twenty years. Some beds have supposedly produced for one hundred years, so choose a place that will not be in the way.

The soil should preferably be light and sandy so that drainage is good. Dig a trench at least one and one-half feet deep and three feet wide. Break up the soil and mix in a lot of organic matter. Well-rotted manure is ideal. Return the loosened, fertilized soil to the trench. The added organic matter should raise the bed soil a few inches above the neighboring soil level.

Space the crowns about a foot apart. For each one, dig a hole about six inches deep in the prepared bed. Fill the hole with water. Make a little seat for the crown by pouring a pile of loose soil about three inches high into the middle of the hole. Set the crown on its seat, untangle the roots, and let them extend down toward the bottom of the hole. Pour in more soil, covering the crown and filling the hole. Tamp the soil down lightly and water a second time. If you plant more than one row of asparagus, make sure the rows are four to six feet apart.

Once your plants are started, water them deeply every week or two in dry summer areas; fertilize heavily with a high-nitrogen mixture each year when you see them putting on a big growth spurt; and mulch when you cut back the foliage in the fall. *Be sure not to cut the foliage until after it turns brown,* for without it the plants will have no food supply for the growing perennial crowns. Cultivate only about one inch into the soil so you do not damage the roots, and pull weeds by hand before they get a good start.

Take no spears the first year, unless your crowns are already three years old. You should be able to harvest spears for at least three weeks the second year, and up to eight or ten weeks the third year. Wait until the spears are about five inches high. Then insert a knife at an angle, and cut the spear off about an inch and a half below the soil surface. When your new spears begin to look spindly and weak, the roots are being overworked, and you should stop cutting and let foliage form for the rest of the season. (Also, if a spear gets more than eight inches tall, it is past its prime for eating, so let it go.) Think of this as living on your interest and not touching your capital. That way, there will be more interest the next year.

Ask your local nursery or green-thumb neighbors about the asparagus pests in your area, and take care of them, as they appear, with the recommended spray or organic techniques. If you do all this, you should have this favorite vegetable of emperors, painters, gourmets, and kings on your table for most of your adult life. And you may come to feel as strongly about it as the French scientist and man of letters, Bernard Fontenelle (1657-1757), who had a passion for asparagus served with oil. His friend, the Cardinal Dubois, had an equally strong passion for asparagus with butter sauce. Receiving a great bundle of asparagus, Fontenelle invited the Cardinal to dinner. Half the asparagus was to be served with oil and half with butter, in honor of the guest. Just before the dinner hour a messenger rushed in to tell Fontenelle that the Cardinal had died suddenly that afternoon in a fit. Fontenelle jumped up and dashed into the kitchen shouting, "All in oil! All in oil!"

Choosing and Storing Asparagus

"Put the water on to boil," says Mrs. Appleyard, "and then go out and cut your asparagus." In other words, the best way to choose asparagus is right from the garden, and the best way to store it is not at all. But if you have no garden and no wild asparagus patch, you may have to make some compromises.

Bunches of fresh asparagus may vary in weight from three-fourths of a pound to two and one-half pounds. Allow five to seven stalks or one-fourth pound per person unless you are dealing with real asparagus lovers. In that case, double the allowance. One pound cut in pieces will equal about two cups cooked asparagus. One package of frozen asparagus will be approximately equal to one small bunch of asparagus. It may weigh only ten to twelve ounces, but will contain less waste.

For most purposes, choose plump, firm, straight stalks whose flower buds are all still tightly closed. For some recipes you will want the slender kind of spring asparagus, called "sprue," which is often found frozen. But it, too, must be fresh and crisp. The stalks should be green for at least two-thirds of their length, the woody white part apparently helping to preserve moisture and freshness.

According to one gourmet, asparagus should always be treated as a bouquet—stood up with its feet in water. In my experience, such treatment does help. If this takes up too much room in your refrigerator, at least wrap the butts of the stalks in damp paper towels before storing in the vegetable crisper. Use as soon as possible.

Getting Asparagus Ready for Cooking

Untie the bunches and wash the asparagus thoroughly. Pick up the spears one by one, the tip in one hand and the butt in the other, and bend each until it breaks naturally. Use the end toward the tip for your recipe, reserving the bases for soup or purée. If the spears are too limp to break, reserve them, too, for cream of asparagus soup or purée, or for recipes where the asparagus will be thoroughly cooked.

Unless asparagus comes straight from the garden bed, you may want to peel it before using. If you think this sounds like too much work, test-cook a single spear to the doneness you like and then see how easy it is to cut. If it seems stringy, then peel at least the lower part of the spears you intend to use. Another way to solve this problem is to cut the spears into bite-size pieces instead of leaving them whole as many recipes suggest.

16

Cooking
Asparagus

Everyone seems to have a favorite method and a favorite cooking time for asparagus. But almost everyone agrees on one rule: the quicker the better. When the Roman Emperor Augustus said he wanted someone's head off *Citius quam asparagi coquintur* (quicker than you can cook asparagus), he meant in a hurry. Asparagus should be what the Italians call *al dente,* and what Americans call fork-tender, tender-crisp, or crunchy-tender—both cultures meaning that the teeth should still have a little pleasant work to do. The one exception is cooking the tougher ends of spears for soup or purée. Then, of course, cook the asparagus as soft as possible.

Common sense dictates another well-accepted rule: fat asparagus takes longer to cook than thin, and bottoms longer than tips. Since the composition of the cooking pan, the type of stove being used, and the freshness of the asparagus can all make a difference, think of the cooking times given here as approximations. Fork the asparagus often as it cooks so that you can take it off the heat at just the right time.

There are three basic cooking methods, of which all the others are variations.

The Puritan or upright method Steam-boil the whole spears in a bunch (some people recommend retying with string after cleaning), standing them upright in about an inch of boiling salted water and cooking them uncovered for five minutes and covered for ten. This

17

method has been around in one form or another since Roman times. It is the only one that gives you whole spears and still takes care of the difference in cooking rate between tip and base. Its disadvantage is that it requires a rather tall pot, but many people solve the problem by using a coffee pot. Special pans are also available for this purpose.

The Epicurean or reclining method Lay the stalks flat in boiling salted water for about ten minutes. Be sure they are no more than two or three stalks deep. This is the easiest method, but takes no account of the fact that tips cook faster than bases. Test spears often as they cook.

Some cooks maintain that you can keep asparagus from getting too soft during this method of cooking if you first blanch the spears, remove them from the water, and dry them on paper towels before returning them to the hot water.

A variation of the reclining method is to cut the spears in three pieces, putting the thickest into the boiling water first, adding the middle segments about halfway through, and adding the tip segments for just the last three minutes or so of the cooking time.

The Oriental or on-the-bias method Cut the spears diagonally into pieces about one and one-half inches long and one-eighth to one-fourth inch thick. Cook them in a hot skillet in butter or cooking oil for three to five minutes, stirring constantly.

Asparagus may also be cooked in a pressure cooker (for about two minutes) or in a microwave oven. A brief table for microwave cooking follows:

> fresh spears in one-fourth cup salted water in a plastic-covered rectangular baking dish—five to six minutes (stir once, rearrange once);
>
> frozen spears (ten ounces) in a one-quart covered baking dish, ice side up—seven to eight minutes (stir twice, rearrange once);
>
> frozen cut (nine ounces) in a one-quart casserole (slit pouch)—five to six minutes (stir twice).

You can vary many of the recipes in this book simply by varying the way you cook the asparagus used in them. Always save your asparagus cooking liquid for soup stock if it is not called for in the recipe itself. Besides plain salted water, you can cook your asparagus in milk, white wine, ale, cider, chicken broth, veal broth, or water containing lemon juice, dill pickle vinegar, cider or white wine vinegar, or creamy French dressing.

As gourmets have often emphasized, asparagus fresh from the garden needs nothing but a quick cooking and the barest and most subtle of dressings. You will not always be able to get garden-fresh asparagus, but I assume that you like asparagus well enough to want to know many ways to prepare it and eat it.

Appetizers

TRIPLE THREAT APPETIZER PLATE

I. The Green—Asparagus Superpurée

AUTUMN'S ASPARAGUS PURÉE (see index)   2 cups
PREPARED HORSERADISH   2 tablespoons
SALT   ⅛ teaspoon or to taste
LEMON JUICE   1 tablespoon

For a very mild dip, Autumn's Asparagus Purée can be used as is. Otherwise, add the last 3 ingredients to purée and chill. Makes about 2 cups.

II. The Pink—Better-than-Liver Pâté

CHICKEN HEARTS and GIZZARDS   2 cups cooked tender
MAYONNAISE   ¼ cup
SOUR CREAM   ⅓ cup
PREPARED HORSERADISH   1 tablespoon
GARLIC POWDER   ¼ teaspoon
ONION SALT   ¼ teaspoon
SALT   to taste

Cut giblets; allow any natural gelatin to cling to the pieces.* Put chopped meat, mayonnaise, and sour cream into blender ⅓ at a time. Blend after each addition to avoid overloading. Add seasonings and blend again thoroughly until pâté spreads easily. Can be left at room temperature and served at once, although flavors will blend better if refrigerated for a while. Will stiffen slightly (taking the form of a mold if desired) when chilled. If it becomes too stiff, add more mayonnaise and blend again. Makes about 2 cups.

*If giblets have been refrigerated in their own broth, some of their natural gelatin may be clinging to them. Although not crucial, this gelatin does improve the consistency of the pâté.

III. The White—Saucy Feta Spread

FETA CHEESE   2 cups crumbled
MAYONNAISE   2 tablespoons
WORCESTERSHIRE SAUCE   8 drops
DILL WEED   2 teaspoons
GARLIC POWDER   dash

Mash all ingredients together thoroughly with a fork. If feta is dry, add more mayonnaise and a little dill pickle vinegar if you have it, and whirl mixture in blender. If spread is too sharp, add softened cream cheese to taste. Chill. Makes about 2 cups.

Arrange the three spreads attractively on a platter with garnishes of parsley and radish roses or cherry tomatoes. Surround with bacon-flavored crackers for the asparagus purée, thinly sliced dill rye or French bread for the pâté, and stone-ground wheat wafers or rice crackers for the feta spread—or find your own favorite combinations.

The use of the term *divan* to mean "with asparagus" may go back to a now-defunct restaurant called the Divan Parisien in New York, which introduced a dish called Chicken Divan. This dish was originally made with broccoli, and the term is sometimes still used in this way, but asparagus seems to be taking over as the more common meaning. By using this name for a dish containing only asparagus purée, I am probably extending its meaning.

DEVILLED EGGS DIVAN

EGGS   12, hard-cooked
ASPARAGUS PURÉE   ¼ cup
MAYONNAISE   2 tablespoons
PARSLEY   ⅛ teaspoon finely chopped
PREPARED MUSTARD   1 teaspoon
CIDER VINEGAR   1 tablespoon*
LEMON JUICE   1½ teaspoons*
SALT   ¾ teaspoon
PAPRIKA   ⅛ teaspoon
PARSLEY   garnish
PITTED BLACK OLIVES   8, sliced

Cool eggs under cold running water, peel, and slice in half lengthwise; remove yolks, and set whites aside. Purée cooked asparagus. If you use any bottoms of stalks, peel them beforehand. Mix purée, mayonnaise, parsley, and seasonings with yolks, mashing them together with a fork or using a blender for making smoother-textured filling. If the color is not pleasing, add green food coloring until the mixture turns a light mint green. Fill egg-white halves with green filling and garnish each with parsley and a ring of black olive. Chill covered until serving time. Makes 24 halves.

If you cook the asparagus in ⅔ water and ⅓ dill pickle vinegar, you may omit lemon juice or cider vinegar.

COLD-ROLLED ASPARAGUS

FRESH ASPARAGUS   1 bunch or 24 spears
DELICATESSEN-STYLE BREAST OF TURKEY
     and HAM   6 thin slices each
SMALL ONION   1, chopped fine
DIJON MUSTARD   1 teaspoon
CAPERS   2 teaspoons chopped
CREAMY, ORANGE FRENCH DRESSING   ½ cup
EGG YOLKS   6, hard-cooked
SALT   to taste
ORANGE   1, sectioned or sliced
PARSLEY   2 tablespoons chopped

Trim asparagus spears to size of ham and turkey slices; cook until crunchy-tender. Divide spears into 12 piles. Mix onion, mustard, and capers with French dressing; thicken to paste with mashed egg yolk, and spread on meat slices, adding salt if needed. If paste is runny, add more egg yolk. Some sauce may be left over (¼ to ½ cup). Roll meat slices around asparagus spears and arrange on a platter; surround with orange slices and sprinkle with parsley. Keep chilled until serving time. Makes 12 appetizers.

GREEN-STUFFED MUSHROOMS

MUSHROOM CAPS   15, half-dollar to silver-dollar size
BUTTER or MARGARINE   3 tablespoons
WATER CHESTNUTS   4 to 5 thinly sliced
PREPARED HORSERADISH   ¼ teaspoon
AUTUMN'S ASPARAGUS PURÉE (see index)   15 tablespoons
BACON SLICES or BACON BITS   8 thin slices or equivalent
BLACK OLIVES   5, sliced

Remove mushroom stems and hollow caps out slightly, saving stems for other uses. Sauté caps flat side down in butter for 2 to 3 minutes; drain. Lay 1 water chestnut slice in the bottom of each cap. Add horseradish to asparagus purée and fill caps with mixture. Soft-cook slices of bacon, slit each lengthwise, and wrap the resulting ribbon of bacon around caps. Secure with half a toothpick if necessary. Or sprinkle tops with bacon bits. Garnish each cap with an olive slice. In a 350° oven, bake about 15 minutes on a rack over a baking pan. (If you set them directly on the pan, they will be too moist to handle as finger food.) Drain and cool briefly on paper towels before serving. Makes 15 appetizers.

NOTE: This can also be served as a vegetable, making 3 to 5 servings as is or by using 4 to 5 giant mushroom caps instead of the 15 smaller ones.

ASPARAGUS AFTER-FIVE SPREAD

CREAM CHEESE   4 ounces softened
AUTUMN'S ASPARAGUS PURÉE (see index)   ½ cup
DRY MUSTARD   ½ teaspoon
SALT   to taste
DILL WEED   ½ teaspoon
HAM   ½ cup finely minced
ASPARAGUS TIPS   12, cooked

Mix cream cheese, asparagus purée, mustard, and other seasonings; blend with ham and chill. Serve garnished with asparagus tips cooked until barely tender. Provide your favorite cracker or toast rounds. Spreads about 30 crackers.

SPARROWGRASS BUTTONS

ARTICHOKE BOTTOMS   12, marinated*
AUTUMN'S ASPARAGUS PURÉE (see index)   12 tablespoons
CHEDDAR or CHESHIRE CHEESE   grated

Drain artichoke bottoms. Put 1 tablespoon of purée on each, and top with the grated cheese. Heat in a buttered baking dish for 10 to 15 minutes at 350° until the cheese is well melted but not hard. Makes 12 appetizers. This dish can also be served as a vegetable with ham, chicken, or roast beef. Count 3 to 4 artichoke bottoms per serving for this use.

*For a blander dish, use plain asparagus purée or unmarinated bottoms.

Raw vegetables have become a regular part of the American cocktail hour and appetizer repertoire. Tiny asparagus tips can be served raw, but whole spears, unless garden fresh and well trimmed, should probably be steamed *briefly* (they must still be crunchy). If the spears must stand on the table any length of time, stand them in crushed ice. Peel bottoms of spears if there is any hint of stringiness. Following are several sauces or dips for cold asparagus. To convert dip to sauce or vice versa, merely thin or thicken as desired, adjusting the seasonings as necessary.

MALTESE MAYONNAISE

ORANGE   1, juice and grated rind
MAYONNAISE

Add the grated rind and juice of an orange to your favorite mayonnaise. Adjust amount of orange juice for consistency desired.

BROWN BUTTER MAYONNAISE

BUTTER   1 cup
EGG YOLKS   4

In heavy saucepan heat butter until nicely browned but not burnt; cool slightly. Beat yolks until thick. Then, while continuing to beat in rotary beater or blender, add 2 tablespoons of the butter, then 2 more tablespoons. After this, add butter in slow, steady stream. Chill. To soften before serving, whip. Makes about 1½ cups.

FIVE-GREENS MAYONNAISE*

FRESH SPINACH LEAVES   10
WATERCRESS LEAVES   2 tablespoons
PARSLEY LEAVES   2 tablespoons
TARRAGON LEAVES   1 tablespoon
AUTUMN'S ASPARAGUS PURÉE (see index)   1 tablespoon
SMALL GREEN ONIONS   2, minced
LEMON JUICE   1 tablespoon
GARLIC POWDER   ⅛ teaspoon
MAYONNAISE   1 cup
SALT   to taste
PARSLEY   2 tablespoons minced

All ingredients should be fresh if possible. Put spinach, watercress, parsley, and tarragon leaves together with the asparagus purée, onion, lemon juice, and garlic powder into a blender and make a smooth paste. Stir this paste into the mayonnaise and mix thoroughly; salt to taste and add parsley. Chill. Makes about 1⅓ cups.

*A modified Sauce Vincent.

EGG AND CURRY DIP

EGGS   2, hard-cooked
MAYONNAISE   ½ cup
PREPARED HORSERADISH   1 teaspoon
DILL PICKLE VINEGAR   1 tablespoon
CURRY POWDER   1 teaspoon
SALT   to taste
GARLIC POWDER   to taste

Mash the eggs thoroughly with a fork. Combine with all other ingredients, blending thoroughly. Adjust consistency by adding more egg or more dill pickle vinegar. Makes about 1 cup.

Vinaigrette is one of the classic ways to eat asparagus. The basic vinaigrette sauce is simply oil and vinegar seasoned with salt and pepper. However, the variations are nearly infinite, depending on the kind and proportion of oil and vinegar used, whether the pepper is freshly ground, and what other herbs and ingredients are added. Lemon or lime juice, for example, is often used instead of vinegar. Jane Grigson, author of the cookbook *Good Things,* favors a little sugar, although James Beard disagrees. Dijon mustard is often added. Here is a good basic recipe from which to depart.

VINAIGRETTE

WHITE WINE VINEGAR or LEMON JUICE   2 tablespoons
OLIVE OIL   6 to 12 tablespoons
SALT   ¼ teaspoon
FRESHLY GROUND PEPPER   to taste
HERBS   to taste*

For best results, beat salt and pepper into ½ the vinegar and ¹/₆ the oil with a wire whisk; add ⅓ more of the oil and beat again; add the remaining ½ of both oil and vinegar and beat for the third time. Not long before serving, add herbs as desired and shake well. If dressing must be stored, store covered in a cool place. Marinate cooked and cooled asparagus spears in this sauce and then serve as they are or with mayonnaise; or serve them plain with sauce poured on them at the table. Makes about 1 cup.

*Chervil, chopped parsley, tarragon, and chives or spring onion tops could be added; or try ¼ teaspoon dry mustard.

CREAM CHEESE SAUCE #1

CREAM CHEESE   8 ounces, whipped
SALT   1 teaspoon
PAPRIKA   1 teaspoon
PREPARED HORSERADISH   1 teaspoon
FRESH LIME JUICE   1 tablespoon
OLIVE OIL   6 tablespoons
CHERVIL   ½ teaspoon

To cream cheese and salt, add remaining ingredients. Then beat until fluffy. Makes about 1 cup.

CREAM CHEESE SAUCE #2

CREAM CHEESE   8 ounces, whipped
SALT   1 teaspoon
EGG YOLKS   2, hard-cooked
DIJON MUSTARD   2 tablespoons plus 1 teaspoon
OIL   ½ cup, drop by drop
LEMON JUICE   to taste
PARSLEY   to taste, chopped

To cream cheese and salt, add remaining ingredients. Blend until sauce is consistency of mayonnaise. Makes about 1½ cups.

TARRAGON SAUCE

SOUR CREAM   1 cup
SUGAR   2 teaspoons
TARRAGON   1 teaspoon
SALT   1 teaspoon or to taste
WHITE WINE VINEGAR   1¼ teaspoons or to taste

Blend all ingredients, adding just enough vinegar to bring to desired sharpness and consistency. Makes about 1 cup.

ANCHOVY AND GARLIC SAUCE

OLIVE OIL   2 tablespoons
ANCHOVY FILLETS   10
GARLIC CLOVE   1, minced
ONION JUICE   1 teaspoon
PARSLEY   ½ cup chopped
OREGANO   2 teaspoons
LEMON JUICE   2 tablespoons
EGG YOLKS   4, hard-cooked

Put oil into small skillet; add anchovies and garlic and cook gently for about 5 minutes until anchovies disintegrate. Gradually add onion juice, parsley, oregano, lemon juice, and mashed egg yolks, stirring constantly. If sauce is too thick, thin with half hot water and half lemon juice; blend in well. Serve cold. Makes less than 1 cup.

Soups
and
Salads

Asparagus soups are traditional favorites. In case you wonder why traditional recipes get modified for modern kitchens, consider this recipe from *The Compleat Housewife* of 1730:

TO MAKE ASPARAGUS SOUP.—Take 12 pounds of lean beef, cut in slices; then put a quarter of a pound of butter in a stewpan over the Fire, and put your Beef in; let it boil up quick till it begins to brown; then put in a pint of brown Ale and a gallon of Water, and cover it close, and let it stew gently for an hour and a half; put in what Spice you like in the stewing, and strain out the Liquor, and scum off all the Fat; then put in some Vermicelli, and some Sallery wash'd and cut small. Half a hundred of Asparagus cut small, Palates boiled tender and cut; put all these in, and let them boil gently till tender. Just as 'tis going up, fry a handful of Spinnage in Butter, and throw in a French Roll.

It is in the soups, incidentally, that you get to use all those asparagus-stalk bottoms you have been told to save for other uses. Here, too, you can use leftover cooked asparagus in almost any form, including creamed and au gratin.

You can make this old favorite without cream, as in this quick recipe, which I call

MILK OF ASPARAGUS SOUP

FRESH ASPARAGUS   1 bunch
MILK   1 quart
PARMESAN CHEESE   ¼ cup grated
BUTTER or MARGARINE   4 tablespoons
SALT   to taste
FRESH CHIVES   3 tablespoons chopped

Chop asparagus, cook until tender, and mash fine or purée in blender. Add milk, Parmesan cheese, butter, and salt. Garnish with chives. Serve hot. Serves 4.

QUICK CREAM OF ASPARAGUS SOUPS

1)   Add Autumn's Asparagus Purée (see index) or plain asparagus purée or leftover Mashed Asparagus (see index) to your favorite basic cream soup recipe, or to leftover white sauce. Adjust consistency with chicken broth if necessary.

2)   Use asparagus cooking liquid instead of water to dilute a canned cream of potato soup, adding leftover cooked asparagus if available.

This recipe is a slightly modernized version of an American recipe from the 1920s.

SETTLEMENT ASPARAGUS SOUP

FRESH ASPARAGUS or STALK BOTTOMS   2 bunches or equivalent
SOUP STOCK   3 pints*
ONION   1 slice
BUTTER or MARGARINE   3 tablespoons
FLOUR   3 tablespoons
SALT   1 teaspoon
PARSLEY   1 teaspoon chopped
MILK and CREAM   ½ cup each or
    HALF-AND-HALF   1 cup
SOUR CREAM   garnish

Peel any woody stalks of asparagus. Cut off tiny tips, if any, and cook about 1 minute until crunchy-tender; drain and set aside. Put stock in soup kettle; add asparagus stalks and onion and boil 30 minutes; drain, reserving stock. Put asparagus and onion through a blender or rub through a sieve. Heat butter; add flour, salt, and parsley. Cook with the hot stock, adding the milk and cream, and the puréed asparagus. Adjust saltiness. Serve in small bowls garnished with a dollop of sour cream and 4 to 5 asparagus tips each. If you have no tips, use a sprig of parsley. Serves 6.

*This can be a genuine old-fashioned stock made by long boiling of beef and beef bones with salt, onion, carrot, celery, tomato, parsley, etc., and enriched by cooking liquids from various vegetables prepared during the week; or you can simply use any meat broth—fresh, canned, or made from bouillon cubes.

VARIATIONS: 1) Substitute 2 cups cream for the butter, flour, milk, and cream (or half-and-half). At last stage, after adding purée and seasonings to stock, put part of soup mixture into double boiler and heat. Beat 4 egg yolks until light. Beat cream into yolks and slowly add to mixture; when mixture coats spoon, pour into main soup. Heat gently and serve. 2) Reduce stock by 1 cup and add 1 cup white wine.

38

This soup was modified from an Italian recipe by Wes Peverieri of Palo Alto, California.

WES'S ASPARAGUS SOUP

FRESH ASPARAGUS   1½ pounds
CHICKEN BROTH   6 cups
BUTTER   ¼ cup
FLOUR   2 tablespoons
BOILED HAM   6 ounces, chopped
SALT and PEPPER   to taste
EGG YOLK   1
WHIPPING CREAM   1 cup
PARMESAN CHEESE   3 heaping tablespoons grated
PARSLEY SPRIGS   6, chopped

Slice asparagus diagonally in 1-inch pieces. Cook in chicken broth until barely tender; drain and keep warm. Reserve broth. Melt butter in saucepan; stir in flour and sauté a few minutes. Gradually add broth and bring to a simmer. Add ham, salt, and pepper; simmer 5 minutes. Beat egg yolk with cream, Parmesan cheese, and parsley; blend into broth and add asparagus. Bring to a simmer and serve. Serves 6.

This recipe was created by Alan Hooker for his famous Ranch House Restaurant in Ojai, California, and is reproduced by permission from his book, *Vegetarian Gourmet Cookery.*

RANCH HOUSE GREEN GODDESS SOUP

FRESH ASPARAGUS   1 small bunch
WATER   ½ cup
FRESH GREEN PEAS   4 cups
MILK   2 quarts, warm
MARJORAM   ¼ teaspoon or 4 sprigs
MINT LEAVES   2
THYME   pinch or 1 sprig
HERB SALT   1¼ tablespoons
LARGE AVOCADO   1
WHIPPING CREAM   garnish
PARSLEY   garnish

Cook asparagus until just done in ¼ cup of the water. Heat, but do not boil, the peas in the rest of the water. Liquefy both asparagus and peas (in a blender), and strain into 1½ quarts of the milk to which you have added marjoram, mint, thyme, and herb salt. Liquefy, without straining, a large avocado in the remaining pint of milk, and add to the mixture. Heat *without boiling,* and serve garnished with unsweetened whipped cream and parsley. Serves 8.

NOTE: The peas keep more of their fresh flavor if they are only heated, not boiled. The soup also should not be boiled after the avocado is added, because overheating creates a strong acid flavor. This has been an extremely popular soup at the Ranch House and many people have been unable to identify the ingredients. It should be light in color.

SOUP SOMEWHAT A LA MOLIÈRE

FRESH ASPARAGUS   1 small bunch or
    CANNED ASPARAGUS TIPS   1 8½-ounce can
GREEN PEAS   1¾ cups cooked
CHICKEN or VEAL STOCK   1½ quarts
CAULIFLOWER   ½ cup cooked
FLOUR   1 tablespoon
CHIVES   1 tablespoon snipped
BUTTER or MARGARINE   1 tablespoon
EGG YOLKS   1 to 2
CREAM   ½ cup
SALT   to taste
SOUR CREAM   garnish
CHICKEN   cooked and shredded

Cook asparagus and peas in stock until just done; drain and save a few asparagus tips for garnish. Force cooked asparagus and peas through sieve or purée in blender with the cooked cauliflower; return to stock. Thicken stock-and-vegetable mixture with flour; add chives and butter and cook 8 to 10 minutes, stirring continually. Pour mixture (somewhat cooled) into yolks and cream beaten together; season to taste. Garnish with asparagus tips, chicken, and chives atop a dollop of sour cream. Serves 6.

ASPARAGUS AND BEAN SPROUT BOUILLON

FRESH ASPARAGUS   2 pounds
CHICKEN BOUILLON   2 quarts
CORNSTARCH   3 tablespoons
DILL WEED   1 teaspoon
BEAN SPROUTS   2 cups
SALT   to taste
FRESHLY GROUND PEPPER   to taste
CHIVES   chopped

Cut asparagus crosswise in ½-inch slices, and simmer until tender in 2 cups of the bouillon. Mix 1 cup bouillon with the cornstarch and stir until smooth. Add remaining bouillon and cornstarch-thickened bouillon to asparagus; add dill weed and bean sprouts. Cook, stirring constantly, until mixture is slightly thick. Season to taste with salt and pepper and garnish with chives. Serves 6 to 8.

FRESH ASPARAGUS   1 pound
SMALL HEAD CAULIFLOWER   1
FRESH PEAS   1 pound
SMALL HEAD LETTUCE   1
GREEN ONION TOPS   1 bunch
FRESH PARSLEY   1 cup chopped or
     NASTURTIUM LEAVES   ½ cup
CHICKEN BOUILLON   2½ quarts
FINE EGG NOODLES   1 cup
LEAN GROUND PORK   1 pound
SALT   to taste
GARLIC POWDER   to taste
CHERVIL   2 tablespoons

Cut asparagus into bite-size pieces, break cauliflower into small florets, shell peas, shred lettuce, and chop green onion tops and parsley. Place in large saucepan with 1 quart bouillon, onion tops, and parsley; simmer, covered, for 15 to 20 minutes or until tender. Add remaining bouillon and noodles, cooking uncovered until noodles are tender. Season pork with salt, garlic powder, and chervil; shape into tiny meatballs, and precook in a skillet over low heat. Add meatballs to soup and simmer 5 minutes more. Adjust seasoning to taste. Serves 6 to 8.

ASPARAGUS SOUP WITH CRAB

CHICKEN STOCK   8 cups
ONION   1, chopped
GARLIC CLOVE   1, minced
GIANT MUSHROOM CAPS or
    CANNED MUSHROOMS   6 or equivalent, thinly sliced*
WHITE WINE   1 cup
FRESH ASPARAGUS   1½ pounds cut in bite-size pieces
CHIVES or GREEN ONION TOPS   2 tablespoons chopped
CRAB MEAT   ½ to ¾ pound flaked
CORNSTARCH   2 teaspoons
COLD WATER
SOY SAUCE   1 tablespoon
EGGS   2

Heat stock and add onion, garlic, and mushroom liquid, if you have any; simmer about 10 minutes. Add wine and return to low boil. Add asparagus, mushrooms, and chives, and continue simmering for about 10 minutes until asparagus is done; then add crab. Combine cornstarch with a little cold water and add to mixture, stirring until it begins to thicken; add soy sauce. Dribble beaten eggs into soup to make egg flowers (soup must not be boiling too hard or this will not work). Adjust seasoning to taste. Serves 8.

*If using canned mushrooms, reserve liquid.

WITH-IT ASPIC

SMALL FRESH ASPARAGUS TIPS   1½ pounds
UNFLAVORED GELATIN   2 envelopes
CHICKEN BROTH   ½ cup*
CONDENSED CREAM OF SHRIMP SOUP   1 10½-ounce can*
DRY WHITE WINE   ½ cup
PREPARED HORSERADISH   1 teaspoon
LEMON JUICE   1 tablespoon
PIMIENTOS   ¼ cup slivered
YOGURT   1 cup
CELERY   1 cup finely diced
GREEN ONION TOPS   3 tablespoons chopped

Remove asparagus tips from stalks and cook until just tender (*al dente*); drain and set aside. Dissolve gelatin in chicken broth; add undiluted shrimp soup, wine, and horseradish. Heat to a near-boil, stirring constantly. When mixture is smooth, remove from heat and add lemon juice; chill until thick as heavy syrup. While mixture is chilling, arrange half the asparagus tips and a few of the pimientos in a pleasing pattern in the bottom of a 1½-quart mold. (For example, arrange tips as "spokes" of a wheel around a ring of pimiento.) Cut rest of tips into bite-size pieces. When mixture is ready, fold in chopped asparagus tips, yogurt, celery, remaining pimientos, and onion tops; pour into mold and chill until firm. At serving time, unmold on plate so that arrangement of tips and pimientos shows. Serves 8 to 10.

If you want a vegetarian aspic, substitute asparagus cooking liquid for the chicken broth, and cream of celery soup for the cream of shrimp.

ASPARAGUS-SHRIMP SALAD TOPPER

FRESH ASPARAGUS   1 pound
SHRIMP   1 pound, cooked
MAYONNAISE   ½ cup
LEMON JUICE   1 tablespoon
WORCESTERSHIRE SAUCE   ½ teaspoon
TABASCO SAUCE   dash
DILL WEED   ¼ teaspoon
DRY MUSTARD   1 teaspoon
SOUR CREAM   1 cup
WORCESTERSHIRE SAUCE   3 to 4 drops
SEASONING MIX   1½ teaspoons*

Cook asparagus until crunchy-tender, cut into small bite-size pieces, and chill. Shrimp should also be cold. Combine first 8 ingredients in bowl. Make sour cream dressing by combining remaining ingredients. Then pour into bowl and mix thoroughly. Chill until needed as a delightful filling for avocado halves, or as a dressing for avocado slices or fresh greens. Makes about 1 quart.

*Seasoning mix is made of 2 tablespoons dried parsley, 2 teaspoons Beau Monde seasoning, 2 teaspoons savory salt, and 1 teaspoon minced garlic.

RED AND GREEN SALAD

FRESH ASPARAGUS SPEARS   12 large or 18 small
SALAD OIL   ½ cup
DILL PICKLE VINEGAR   ¼ cup
SALT   1 teaspoon
DRY MUSTARD   1 teaspoon
GARLIC POWDER   ⅛ teaspoon
ONION   2 teaspoons grated
TONGUE, HAM, TURKEY, or PROSCIUTTO   6 thin slices
MAYONNAISE   to taste
ALFALFA SPROUTS   1½ cups or to taste
RED LETTUCE LEAVES   6
RADISHES   to taste
BLACK OLIVES   to taste

Cook asparagus until barely tender; cool and put into refrigerator dish. Mix next 6 ingredients for marinade, pour over asparagus, and refrigerate at least 1 hour. Just before serving, remove from refrigerator and drain spears. Spread each slice of meat with mayonnaise and sprinkle with a layer of alfalfa sprouts. Roll 2 large or 3 small asparagus spears in each meat slice. Serve on a lettuce leaf with radish roses, olives, and remaining sprouts. Makes 6 salads.

JAPANESE-STYLE ASPARAGUS SALAD

FRESH ASPARAGUS   1 to 1½ pounds
VEGETABLE OIL   2 tablespoons
SESAME SEEDS   2 tablespoons
VINEGAR   3 tablespoons
SUGAR   3 tablespoons
SOY SAUCE   1 teaspoon
SALT   to taste (optional)

Steam asparagus for 3 to 4 minutes until barely tender. Meanwhile, heat oil and sesame seeds until seeds are light brown; remove from heat and let cool. Add vinegar, sugar, soy sauce, and salt (if desired), and blend well to make a sauce. Drain asparagus, cool in cold water, and drain again. Cut on bias into ¾-inch pieces. Pour sauce over all, making sure all pieces are coated. Chill and serve. Serves 4.

SPÁRGASALÁTA

ASPARAGUS TIPS   1 pound
SALAD OIL   ½ cup
MUSHROOMS   1 pound
SMALL GREEN TOMATOES   6*
MEDIUM RED TOMATOES   4, cut into wedges
CAULIFLOWER   ½ head separated into florets
GHERKINS   4, sliced
LETTUCE   ½ head shredded
RED CABBAGE   ½ head shredded
WHITE WINE VINEGAR   3 tablespoons
LEMON JUICE   3 tablespoons
SALT and PEPPER   to taste
OLIVE OIL   as needed

If using fresh asparagus, cook tips for 3 to 4 minutes. Then plunge them into cold water for several minutes; drain. Sauté mushrooms and green tomatoes in oil at low heat for about 5 minutes; remove from heat and cool. Reserve any remaining oil. Combine with asparagus tips, red tomatoes, cauliflower, and gherkins, and toss lightly with lettuce and cabbage. Dress with vinegar, lemon juice, salt, and pepper mixed with the oil left from cooking mushrooms. Add olive oil as needed. Chill through and serve. Serves 4.

If fresh green tomatoes are not available, use canned green tomatoes or canned tomatillos.

SPARROWGRASS TOSSER

FRESH ASPARAGUS   1 pound or 2 cups chopped
GREEN LETTUCE   ½ head or 4 cups torn
RED LETTUCE   ½ head or 4 cups torn
CELERY   ½ cup sliced
JERUSALEM ARTICHOKE   ½ cup diced*
GREEN ONIONS   ¼ cup, including tops
CARROT   1, thinly sliced
SALAD OIL   ½ cup
WHITE WINE VINEGAR   2 tablespoons
LEMON JUICE   2 tablespoons
PARSLEY   1 tablespoon
DRY MUSTARD   ½ teaspoon
TABASCO SAUCE   4 drops
SALT   1 teaspoon
SUGAR   1 teaspoon
PAPRIKA   1 teaspoon
EGG YOLK   1, hard-cooked and crumbled
PICKLED BEET   slivered

Cook asparagus until barely tender; drain, cut into bite-size pieces, and chill. Just before serving, combine with lettuce, celery, Jerusalem artichoke, onion, and carrot. Mix next 9 ingredients to make dressing; shake well and pour over salad; toss lightly. Garnish with egg and beet. Serves 6 to 8.

If you cannot find Jerusalem artichokes in your area, you can use water chestnuts or jicama root in the same way.

ASPARAGUS IN PEPPER RINGS

ASPARAGUS SPEARS   16 to 24*
CREAMY, ORANGE FRENCH
  DRESSING   enough to marinate spears
LARGE SWEET RED PEPPER   1
LETTUCE LEAVES
MAYONNAISE   to taste
FRESH MUSHROOMS   8, sliced
MARINATED ARTICHOKE HEARTS   4
RADISHES   4, made into flowers
DEVILLED EGGS DIVAN (see index)   8 halves
CANNED BABY CORN   optional

If using fresh asparagus, trim well and cook until barely tender. Marinate spears in dressing for at least 1 hour in refrigerator. Slice red pepper, remove seeds, and make 4 good rings. Divide asparagus spears into 4 bundles and put each bundle through a red-pepper ring. Arrange on lettuce leaves, with a small dollop of mayonnaise on each side of the ring. On each plate, put some mushroom slices, an artichoke heart, a radish flower, and 2 halves of devilled eggs. To make a really special salad, give each plate a few ears of corn. Makes 4 salads.

*White asparagus would be good in this salad.

Add crunchy-tender tiny asparagus tips to your own favorite chicken salad recipe, or try this one, which can also be served on chow mein noodles as a main lunch or dinner course.

CHICKEN SALAD DIVAN

TINY ASPARAGUS TIPS   1 cup
CHICKEN   4 cups cooked, boned, and shredded
ONION   ¼ cup finely chopped
CELERY   ½ cup chopped
JICAMA ROOT   ½ cup sliced*
WALNUTS or ALMONDS   ½ cup broken or sliced
FRESH MUSHROOMS   1 cup sliced
MAYONNAISE   2 cups
GARLIC POWDER   ¼ teaspoon
SALT   to taste
RED LETTUCE LEAVES
PIMIENTOS   sliced
FRESH PARSLEY or WATERCRESS   garnish

If using fresh asparagus, cook until crunchy-tender. Then combine first 10 ingredients. Mix well and chill in refrigerator for several hours before serving. At serving time, place mixture on lettuce leaves and garnish with pimiento and parsley. Serves 8.

*Jerusalem artichoke or water chestnuts may be used instead.

ASPIC AUX RAISINS

LEMON GELATIN   1 6-ounce package
LEMON JUICE   2 tablespoons
FROZEN CONCENTRATED ORANGE JUICE   2 tablespoons
DRY MUSTARD   ¼ teaspoon
PAPRIKA   ¼ teaspoon
ASPARAGUS TIPS   1 cup
SEEDLESS GREEN GRAPES   2 cups
WATER CHESTNUTS   1 cup or 1 6-ounce can, diced
FRESH ORANGE SECTIONS   1 cup peeled and cut up or
       MANDARIN ORANGE SECTIONS   1 11-ounce can, drained
RED LETTUCE LEAVES
HONEYED MAYONNAISE   1 cup*

Follow package directions for making gelatin, except add lemon and orange juice to the cold water and use 4 tablespoons less cold water than gelatin directions call for. Add mustard and paprika to dissolved gelatin, and chill to set. Meanwhile, if using fresh asparagus tips, cook until barely crunchy-tender; if frozen, thaw; if canned, chill. Cut grapes in half. When gelatin is nearly set, add the grapes, asparagus, water chestnuts, and orange sections; chill until firm. At serving time place portions on lettuce and top with honeyed mayonnaise. Serves 6 to 8.

To make honeyed mayonnaise, whip 2 tablespoons honey and ½ teaspoon onion juice into 1 cup mayonnaise.

BEETS DRESS ASPARAGUS

FRESH ASPARAGUS   1 bunch
APPLE CIDER VINEGAR   ¼ cup
SALAD OIL   ¾ cup
DRY MUSTARD   ¼ teaspoon
SALT   ½ teaspoon
GREEN ONION   2 tablespoons diced
GORGONZOLA or BLUE CHEESE   2 tablespoons crumbled
BEETS   ½ cup cooked and diced
EGGS   6 to 8, hard-cooked
RED LETTUCE LEAVES
RED ONION RINGS   garnish
BLACK OLIVES   garnish

Cook well-trimmed asparagus until crunchy-tender; drain and chill thoroughly. Make dressing base of vinegar, oil, mustard, and salt; blend well. Stir in onion, cheese, beets, and 1 diced egg. Arrange asparagus on a chilled platter with lettuce around the edge. Slice remaining eggs and arrange around asparagus with onion rings and olives. Sprinkle with dressing and place remaining dressing on table. Serves 4 to 6.

ASPARAGUS SPOKES

FILLING FOR DEVILLED EGGS DIVAN (see index)   2 cups
FRESH GREEN ASPARAGUS   1 bunch
WHITE ASPARAGUS   1 15½-ounce can
RED LETTUCE
ICEBERG LETTUCE
ROMAINE LETTUCE
FRESH SPINACH   if available
BLACK OLIVES   sliced
EGGS   6, hard-cooked and quartered
RADISHES   6, sliced
CHIVES   ½ cup finely chopped
PARSLEY   ½ cup chopped
VINAIGRETTE SAUCE (see index)   to taste
ROMANO CHEESE   ½ cup grated

Make egg filling and chill. Cook green asparagus until crunchy-tender. Use only top 2 inches of spears and peel if there is any hint of toughness. Drain and chill. Drain and chill white asparagus. Just before serving time, arrange greens on chilled platter. Mound egg filling in center of platter and garnish with olive rings. Arrange asparagus spears like spokes of wheel around mound of egg filling, alternating white and green spears. Arrange eggs, radishes, and remaining olives attractively between asparagus spokes. Sprinkle with chives and parsley, and pour Vinaigrette Sauce over all but center mound. Sprinkle with cheese and serve with extra Vinaigrette Sauce. Serves 6.

GREEN SEAS MEDLEY

Green Seas Dressing

SHRIMP   1 4½-ounce can
ROSÉ WINE   ¼ cup
SOUR CREAM   ½ cup
MAYONNAISE   ½ cup
DILL   ⅛ teaspoon
SALT   ½ teaspoon
CUCUMBER   ½ cup peeled and grated
RIPE AVOCADO   1, mashed
LEMON JUICE   2 tablespoons

Prepare dressing ahead of time. Drain shrimp and reserve liquid for shrimp-flavored biscuits (see below). Pour rosé over shrimp; cover and refrigerate for several hours. Add sour cream, mayonnaise, dill, salt, and cucumber to avocado. Drain off 2 tablespoons shrimp-wine mixture and add lemon juice. Combine shrimp and avocado mixtures and chill through. Makes about 2½ cups.

FRESH or FROZEN ASPARAGUS SPEARS   24
ROSÉ WINE   ½ cup
RED WINE VINEGAR   ¼ cup
WHITE WINE VINEGAR   ¼ cup
OLIVE OIL   1½ cups
GARLIC SALT   1 teaspoon
SALT   1 teaspoon
DRY MUSTARD   1 teaspoon

PAPRIKA   1 teaspoon
ONION SALT   1 teaspoon
SMALL ZUCCHINIS   3 cups cut lengthwise and then diagonally
CARROTS   2 cups peeled and sliced diagonally
CELERY   1 cup diced
RED LETTUCE LEAVES
GREEN LETTUCE LEAVES
CHERRY TOMATOES   1 basket

Cook asparagus until crunchy-tender; drain and slice diagonally. Make marinade of next 9 ingredients. Pour over asparagus, zucchini, and carrot slices and refrigerate, covered, for about 4 hours, stirring occasionally. When nearly ready to serve, drain, and stir in celery. Arrange lettuce leaves around edges of platter, alternating red and green; mound marinated vegetables in middle; surround with cherry tomatoes. Serve with dressing. Serves 6.

Serve Green Seas Medley alone or with hot or cold roast beef or cold chicken; but always serve it with shrimp-flavored biscuits, prepared as follows: substitute shrimp liquid for ⅓ of water in biscuit mix recipe. Add ½ cup grated medium-sharp cheddar cheese and ⅛ teaspoon garlic powder to biscuit flour. When biscuit rounds are ready on baking sheet, make dent or well in top for dab of butter, which will bake in. Bake as usual.

This substantial salad was developed by Susan Eastwood of Burlingame, California. It can also be served as an appetizer or as the main course for a luncheon or supper, if served with a cream soup and hot bread.

ESPÁRRAGOS Y SEVICHE

FRESH LIME JUICE   from 8 limes
OLIVE OIL   8 tablespoons
ANCHOVY PASTE   1 tablespoon
MEDIUM WHITE ONION   1, thinly sliced
CHERVIL or CHINESE PARSLEY   2 tablespoons
GARLIC CLOVE   1, crushed
FRESHLY GROUND PEPPER   to taste
BEAU MONDE SEASONING   1 tablespoon*
FRESH ASPARAGUS TIPS   1 pound
FRESH SOLE or WHITE FISH FILLET   3½ pounds
RED LETTUCE and OTHER GREENS   crisp
PIMIENTOS   1 4-ounce jar

Combine first 8 ingredients in a pint jar and shake well or put through blender. Steam asparagus tips barely 5 minutes, drain, plunge into cold water, drain again, and put aside in a bowl to cool. Cut fish into bite-size pieces and place in second bowl. Shake lime juice mixture again. Pour part over the asparagus and part over the fish to barely cover. Cover both bowls and refrigerate for 5 to 6 hours. Turn fish occasionally in the lime-juice mixture (the lime juice pickles or "cooks" the fish). Arrange salad greens on a serving plate. Spoon fish onto greens with slotted spoon and arrange drained asparagus tips over fish. Garnish with pimiento strips and serve. Serves about 8.

*Or mix celery salt, onion powder, and MSG (or salt) to taste.

58

Vegetable Course

This purée is the basis of several recipes in *The Sparrowgrass Cookbook,* but it can also be used alone as a mild dip or sauce for other vegetables; spiced up as a livelier dip (see index); or mixed with equal parts hollandaise sauce as an exquisite sauce for omelettes or quiches (see index), for cauliflower and other vegetables, or for certain meats and fish.

AUTUMN'S ASPARAGUS PURÉE

FRESH ASPARAGUS   1 bunch or
    FROZEN ASPARAGUS   1 10-ounce package
SALT   to taste
LEMON JUICE   from ½ lemon
MAYONNAISE   ½ tablespoon
WHIPPED COTTAGE CHEESE   ½ cup*

Cook cut-up asparagus until soft in salted water containing the lemon juice. If you use bottoms of any spears, peel them first, for otherwise you may have to sieve the purée. Drain carefully and purée in blender with other ingredients. Adjust saltiness and whirl again briefly. If the color is not pleasing, blend in a few drops of green food coloring. Makes about 2 cups.

If you cannot find whipped cottage cheese, use ricotta or put ordinary creamed cottage cheese through the blender, adding a little half-and-half if needed.

Use this French way with asparagus as a side dish with meats, just as you would use mashed potatoes. It is a good use for leftover asparagus and can also be a layer in a casserole.

MASHED ASPARAGUS

AUTUMN'S ASPARAGUS PURÉE (see index) or
     ORDINARY ASPARAGUS PURÉE   ½ cup*
HALF-AND-HALF   1 tablespoon
BUTTER or MARGARINE   1 tablespoon

Heat gently, preferably in a double boiler, and serve. Makes 1 serving.

*To make ordinary asparagus purée, put soft-cooked, salted asparagus through a blender.

BICENTENNIAL RECIPE

One of the earliest surviving American recipes for asparagus is Ambushed Asparagus, or Asparagus in Ambush. In all of the several versions the idea is the same: hard rolls have their tops cut off, are hollowed out and filled with creamed asparagus, heated briefly in the oven, and served garnished with tiny asparagus tips—or with spears stuck into holes in the top so that they look as if they are growing. One version calls for a pint of cream, which may give you an idea why the recipe seldom appears in modern cookbooks. One modernizer suggests using hollandaise sauce instead of the cream sauce, and a strip of pimiento for garnish. My own modern version is below.

AMBUSHED ASPARAGUS

FROZEN PATTY SHELLS or HARD DINNER ROLLS   6
BUTTER or MARGARINE
FRESH ASPARAGUS   1 bunch or
    FROZEN ASPARAGUS   1 10-ounce package
CHICKEN or VEAL BROTH   salted
WINE/CREAM SAUCE (see index)   2 cups
NUTMEG   to taste

Bake frozen patty shells as directed, or cut tops off rolls and hollow out centers.* Brush cut surfaces with butter, and toast under broiler. Cook asparagus until crunchy-tender in broth; cut into bite-size pieces. Meanwhile make Wine/Cream Sauce. When asparagus is done, combine with sauce; add nutmeg. Fill patty shells or rolls with mixture, replace tops; brush tops with butter, and return briefly to oven. Serve immediately with leftover sauce. If any sauce is left after the meal, it will make a good omelette filling or a good addition to many cream soups. Serves 3.

*Save crumbs for your bird feeder, to extend soup stock, or for other recipes.

ASPARAGUS AND GREEN TOMATO STIR-FRY

GREEN TOMATOES   1 heaping basket, plum-size, or equivalent
ONION   ½ large or 1 medium, chopped coarsely
BACON GREASE   2 tablespoons
FRESH ASPARAGUS   2 pounds of
     tender portions sliced thin diagonally
BUTTER or MARGARINE   1 dab
SALT   1 teaspoon
DILL PICKLE VINEGAR   2 tablespoons
SUGAR   sprinkle (optional)

Quarter green tomatoes or cut them up coarsely if larger than plum-size. Sauté onion in bacon grease until golden. Turn up heat; add asparagus, tomato, butter, and salt; stir-fry about 1 minute. Add dill pickle vinegar; cover and cook until asparagus is just crunchy-tender (2 to 3 minutes at most with small asparagus). Adjust tartness by adding a sprinkle of sugar; or add grated Monterey jack or cheddar cheese, or prefried crumbles of hamburger, or both, during last stage of cooking. Serve at once. Serves 4 to 6.

ASPARAGUS JICAMA

FRESH ASPARAGUS   2½ pounds
MEDIUM JICAMA ROOT   1, quartered and sliced thin
BUTTER   2 tablespoons
FLOUR   2 tablespoons
SALT   ½ teaspoon
ANGOSTURA BITTERS   ¼ teaspoon
MILK   1½ cups
SOURDOUGH FRENCH BREAD CRUMBS   buttered

Cook asparagus until crunchy-tender and cut into bite-size lengths. Butter a shallow baking dish and in it arrange the asparagus and jicama root in alternate layers. Melt butter on low heat and blend in the flour, salt, and bitters; slowly stir in milk and bring to a boil while stirring. When thick, pour over asparagus. Top with bread crumbs and bake for 25 minutes at 350°. Serves 4.

SPARROWGRASS MEDLEY

FRESH ASPARAGUS   1 bunch, trimmed
CAULIFLOWER   1 head separated into bite-size florets
CREAM CHEESE SAUCE #2 (see index)   1 cup
SWISS CHEESE   1 cup grated
TOMATO WEDGES   to taste
DEVILLED EGGS DIVAN (see index)   4 eggs
FRESH PARSLEY   garnish

Cook asparagus and cauliflower until just crunchy-tender. Plunge asparagus quickly into cold water, then drain. Mound cauliflower in center of a large ovenproof serving platter. Arrange asparagus spears around cauliflower. Make sauce, pour over cauliflower and asparagus, and sprinkle cheese over all. Heat in oven until cheese melts; remove. Arrange tomato wedges and devilled eggs between asparagus spears. Garnish with parsley and serve at once. Serves 4 to 6.

DEEP-FRIED ASPARAGUS
WITH SHRIMP-FLAVORED BREAD CRUMBS

FRESH ASPARAGUS   2 bunches
LEMON JUICE
EGG   1
MILK   3 tablespoons
SALT   dash
PEPPER   dash
CAYENNE   dash
SHRIMP-FLAVORED BREAD CRUMBS (see index)
NONSMOKING OIL

Cook asparagus until barely tender; drain and cut into 2-inch pieces.
Marinate in lemon juice for about 1 hour. Meanwhile, beat egg with
milk and seasonings to make batter. Drain asparagus *thoroughly* in
paper towels. Roll each piece in bread crumbs, then in batter, and again
in crumbs. Fry in deep fat at about 370° for only 2 or 4 minutes or just
until asparagus comes to top of oil and is golden brown. Drain and serve
with various sauces or plain as an accompaniment to meat. Serves 6.

ASPARAGUS TEMPURA

ASPARAGUS SPEARS
FLOUR

Coat barely cooked asparagus spears in flour, then dip in a tempura batter. You can use a tempura batter mix or make your own as follows:

Tempura Batter

FLOUR   1 cup
WATER   1 cup
EGG   1
SALT   dash
SUGAR   1 teaspoon
BAKING POWDER   ½ teaspoon
COOKING OIL

Mix first 6 ingredients with eggbeater; then let stand in refrigerator until thick as whipping cream. If it is too thick, thin with water. Cook coated spears in oil until they are hot through and batter has formed a golden case around each one. Oil should be at least 2 inches deep. Test its temperature by dropping a little ball of batter into it; batter should sink and then rise to the surface quickly, sizzling gently. Spears should not be crowded in pan. Drain and serve at once with shrimp tempura or with other vegetables prepared the same way, especially carrots and mushrooms. Serve with a sauce to dip them in.* Allow about 6 spears per person if asparagus is the only vegetable used.

*You can make a dipping sauce ahead of time with soy sauce, vinegar, sherry, sugar to taste, and chicken broth or bouillon. Serve hot.

This old favorite was reportedly invented by a famous gastronome, the Marquis de Cussy, in order to be able to drink wine with asparagus. (Traces of sulfur found in asparagus may spoil the flavor of some wines. The cheese somehow counteracts or neutralizes the sulfur.) De Cussy recommended a glass of old Alicante as the wine of choice for this great dish.

ASPARAGUS AU GRATIN

FRESH, FROZEN, or CANNED
  ASPARAGUS   2 pounds or equivalent
ASPARAGUS COOKING LIQUID   ½ cup
FLOUR   2 tablespoons
BUTTER or MARGARINE   2 tablespoons
MILK   1 cup
GRUYÈRE, SWISS, or CHEDDAR CHEESE   1 cup grated*
SOURDOUGH FRENCH BREAD CRUMBS   1 cup soft
BUTTER   1½ tablespoons, melted
PAPRIKA   garnish

Remove tough parts of asparagus, cut tops into bite-size pieces, and cook until barely tender. Make sauce using next 4 ingredients. When thick, stir in cheese and heat gently until melted. Combine sauce and asparagus, and pour into buttered baking dish. Sprinkle with crumbs; sprinkle crumbs with butter, and then with a little paprika. Place dish under broiler until crumbs are golden brown. Serve at once. Serves 4 to 6.

*If you are tired of asparagus au gratin as you know it, try some different cheeses.

A TANGY VARIATION: Cut and cook asparagus as above; arrange in shallow buttered baking dish. Make a sauce of 1 cup sour cream, ¼ cup mayonnaise, 2 tablespoons lemon juice, and 1 tablespoon horseradish; spoon over asparagus. Lay thin slices of Monterey jack cheese on top and sprinkle casserole with grated Parmesan. Put under broiler just until bubbly.

CREAMED ASPARAGUS

FRESH ASPARAGUS   2 pounds cut up
WINE/CREAM SAUCE (see index)   1½ cups
TOAST, CROUSTADES, or ENGLISH MUFFINS

Cook asparagus until just tender. Drain thoroughly and combine with cream sauce. Serve on toast, croustades, or hot buttered English muffins. Add chipped beef for a variation. Serves 6.

WHITE ASPARAGUS, BELGIAN STYLE

FRESH or CANNED WHITE ASPARAGUS   2 pounds or equivalent
EGGS   4, hard-cooked
BUTTER   1 cup, melted
PARSLEY   2 tablespoons minced
LEMON JUICE   1 tablespoon or
     NUTMEG   ⅛ teaspoon
DRY MUSTARD   1 teaspoon (optional)
CHIVES   1 tablespoon minced (optional)
SALT and WHITE PEPPER   to taste

Cook fresh asparagus until just fork-tender or heat canned asparagus gently in juice from can. Drain thoroughly on paper towel and place on hot serving platter. Mash up eggs in small bowl, mix in other ingredients, and serve in sauceboat beside the asparagus. Serves 4.

SPARROWGRASS ARTICHOKES

LARGE ARTICHOKES   8
LEMON JUICE   from ½ lemon or
     WHITE WINE VINEGAR   1 tablespoon
SALT   2 tablespoons
OIL   2 tablespoons
FRESH ASPARAGUS   3 to 4 bunches or 70 to 80 spears
FRESH TOMATO SAUCE or PIQUANT PECAN SAUCE (see index) or
     THOUSAND ISLAND DRESSING   2 cups
SALT

Wash and drain artichokes. Cut off stems so they sit flat; break off small, tough outer leaves; and cut off top of each artichoke, leaving leaves about 1½ inches tall. Set artichokes in large cooking pot and half-cover them with water. Add lemon juice, salt, and oil. Bring to boil and boil for 30 to 45 minutes, depending on size of artichokes. Meanwhile, cook asparagus until just crunchy-tender (spears must be able to stand upright); trim to the top 2 inches, saving the rest for another use. Season as desired, and keep warm. Keep sauce hot. When artichokes are done, drain them upside down until cool enough to handle. Take out centers and scrape out hearts with a spoon. Sprinkle with salt and keep hot. Fill artichokes with sauce, stand asparagus tips upright in the sauce, and arrange the filled chokes on small platter. Serve with extra sauce. Serves 8.

This variation on the Polish way with asparagus was invented by Shera Thompson of Flagstaff, Arizona.

ASPARAGUS POLONAISE SHERA

FRESH ASPARAGUS   2 pounds
BACON SLICES   6
BREAD CRUMBS   ⅔ cup dry
BUTTER or MARGARINE   2 tablespoons
GARLIC CLOVE   1, crushed
SALT   to taste
LEMON JUICE   from 1 lemon
EGG   1, hard-cooked and sieved
PARSLEY   to taste
DOMESTIC PARMESAN CHEESE   2 tablespoons grated

Trim away all tough parts of asparagus, peel if necessary, and cook until fork-tender. Fry bacon until it is crisp but not at all burnt; remove bacon and crumble. Meanwhile, brown bread crumbs in bacon fat; add butter and garlic. Drain and salt asparagus and place on heated platter. Pour lemon juice over asparagus and garnish with crumbs, bacon, egg, parsley, and cheese. If desired, place under broiler just long enough to melt cheese. Serves 4.

ASPARAGUS PATTIES

FRESH, FROZEN, or CANNED ASPARAGUS   1 bunch or equivalent
GREEN ONIONS   4, finely chopped or
    MEDIUM YELLOW ONION   1, finely chopped
EGGS   2, lightly beaten
WHEAT GERM or BRAN   ⅓ to ½ cup
PREPARED HORSERADISH   1 teaspoon
MONTEREY JACK or CHEDDAR CHEESE   ¼ cup grated
SALT   1 teaspoon
JICAMA ROOT or ALMONDS   1 tablespoon
    finely chopped or slivered

Chop cooked asparagus into ¼-inch pieces and put in bowl; put in all other ingredients and mix well. You will not be able to form patties with your hands; use a large spoon to drop them on oiled grill or into frying pan. If patties seem likely to crumble, sprinkle with more wheat germ or cornflake crumbs just before turning. Brown on both sides; then cook covered 5 to 8 minutes. Gourmets advise serving with button mushrooms, sweetbreads, and a bottle of chablis or Montrachet. Serves 6.

This is the classic sauce for asparagus and is essentially French, in spite of its Dutch-sounding name. Here are four versions, which you can modify for your own tastes. Note the two remedies for curdling among the hollandaise recipes.

CLASSIC HOLLANDAISE

BUTTER   ½ cup
EGG YOLKS   2
LEMON JUICE or VINEGAR   1 teaspoon
WATER   ⅓ cup, boiling
SALT   to taste
WHITE PEPPER   to taste

Divide butter into 3 parts. In the top of a double boiler, combine 1 part of the butter, both egg yolks, and the lemon juice. Whisk, heating gently, until butter is melted. Add the second butter, still stirring; when mixture thickens, add the third. When all is well mixed, gradually add the boiling water, still whisking constantly. Cook over hot (not boiling) water 1 to 2 minutes. Season to taste with salt and pepper. If the sauce curdles, beat in 2 tablespoons boiling water or 2 tablespoons heavy sweet cream. Makes about 1 cup.

QUASI-HOLLANDAISE

BUTTER or MARGARINE   ¼ cup plus 2 tablespoons
FLOUR   2 tablespoons
RICH MILK   ¾ cup, scalded
SALT and WHITE PEPPER   to taste
EGG YOLKS   3
LEMON JUICE or VINEGAR   1 tablespoon

Melt 2 tablespoons butter and blend with flour. Gradually add milk, stirring constantly, and season with salt and pepper. When mixture boils, remove from heat and add egg yolks, one at a time. After each yolk, add ⅓ of the butter, bit by bit, still stirring. Stir in lemon juice. Makes about 1 cup.

MODERN HOLLANDAISE

BUTTER or MARGARINE   ½ cup
LARGE EGG YOLKS   3
SALT and WHITE PEPPER   to taste
LEMON JUICE   1 tablespoon

Cut butter into 6 to 8 pieces and put into heavy little saucepan with egg yolks. Over very low heat, stir yolks and butter together until butter melts and mixture thickens. Add salt, pepper, and lemon juice and stir with whisk. If mixture curdles, add an ice cube and beat with whisk until smooth. Keep warm until ready to serve. Makes about 1 cup.

76

HOLLANDAISE IN A BLENDER

EGG YOLKS   3
LEMON JUICE   2 tablespoons
SALT   ¼ teaspoon
CAYENNE   dash
BUTTER or MARGARINE   ½ cup, melted and *hot*

Put first 4 ingredients into blender; blend briefly. With motor on high speed, gradually add butter. Serve immediately or keep warm by setting blender top in hot water. Makes about 1 cup.

Maltese sauce is a variant of hollandaise sauce and so is essentially a hot mayonnaise. Escoffier is supposed to have used one-half pound of butter per two egg yolks in such sauces.

MALTESE SAUCE

Replace the lemon juice or vinegar in your favorite hollandaise recipe with orange juice, and add some grated orange rind. *Or,* just before serving, add 1 teaspoon grated orange rind and the juice of one small orange for each cup of hollandaise sauce. Use a blood orange if possible. Adjust consistency as desired by varying the proportion of butter.

MUSHROOM SAUCE

FRESH MUSHROOMS   1 cup sliced
BUTTER or MARGARINE   1 tablespoon
LEMON JUICE   2 teaspoons
EGG   1, lightly beaten
MILK   1 cup
DRY MUSTARD   1 teaspoon
CHIVES   1 tablespoon minced
SALT   1 teaspoon
PREPARED HORSERADISH   1 teaspoon
SWISS CHEESE   1 cup grated

Sauté mushrooms about 10 minutes or until tender in butter and lemon juice. Put egg, milk, mustard, chives, and salt in top of double boiler; stir over hot water until mixture thickens slightly. Add horseradish and cheese and cook until thick, stirring constantly; stir in mushrooms. Serve over hot cooked asparagus. Makes 1½ cups.

CAPER SAUCE

To each cup of mayonnaise or hollandaise sauce, add 3½ tablespoons drained capers and 1 teaspoon finely chopped chervil or parsley. Or try this one:

BUTTER or MARGARINE   4 tablespoons
FLOUR   4 tablespoons
CAPERS   1 tablespoon drained and chopped
APPLE CIDER VINEGAR   2 tablespoons
DILL WEED   1 teaspoon
SALT and PEPPER   to taste
CHICKEN or VEAL BROTH   1 cup

As butter heats in saucepan over low flame, gradually add flour and stir constantly until smooth and golden brown. Add capers, vinegar, dill, and seasonings (go easy on salt), still stirring. Add broth and simmer 10 minutes. Serve hot with cooked asparagus. Makes about 1¼ cups.

SEMI-POMPADOUR SAUCE

BUTTER or MARGARINE   ½ cup
GROUND CLOVES   small pinch
CINNAMON   small pinch
SALT   to taste
CAYENNE   few grains
EGG YOLKS   3
SHERRY   1 tablespoon
FLOUR   1 level teaspoon
NUTMEG   garnish

In the top of a double boiler, melt butter. Add cloves, cinnamon, salt, and cayenne. Beat egg yolks carefully with sherry. Stir in alternate portions of the egg-sherry mixture and flour. Stir constantly over hot water until sauce begins to thicken. Serve immediately over hot asparagus with a dusting of nutmeg. Serves 4.

LOS TRANCOS SAUCE

BUTTER or MARGARINE   ¼ cup
SMALL ONION   1, minced
BAY LEAF or CALIFORNIA BAY LEAF   1
SALT and WHITE PEPPER   to taste
FLOUR   3 tablespoons
CHICKEN or VEAL STOCK   2 cups
NUTMEG   pinch
EGG YOLKS   2
LEMON JUICE   1 tablespoon
PIMIENTO   1 tablespoon chopped
BLACK OLIVES   1 tablespoon chopped

In 3 tablespoons of the butter, sauté onion until tender with bay leaf, salt, and pepper. Stir in the flour without lumping, gradually add stock, and cook until thickened, stirring constantly. Add nutmeg, simmer 5 minutes, and remove bay leaf. Beat egg yolks until frothy and yellow, and add lemon juice. Pour a little of the heated sauce into this. Then gradually stir egg mixture into sauce. Cook in top of double boiler, stirring constantly until thickened; then add remaining butter, pimiento, and olives. Heat through and serve over asparagus. Makes about 2½ cups.

FLEMISH SAUCE

EGG   1 per person, soft-cooked*
BUTTER   2 tablespoons per person, melted
SALT and LEMON PEPPER   to taste

Just before serving, mash eggs and butter together and season with salt and lemon pepper; place in bowl beside platter of hot asparagus. *Or,* serve each person an egg and a little container of melted butter; provide the seasonings on the table and let each person mix his or her own sauce or dip the asparagus first into the butter and then into the runny egg yolk.

*Yolk should still be quite runny.

A DUTCH VARIATION: Make the egg hard-cooked and use mustard and oil (with salt, pepper, or lemon pepper as desired) instead of the melted butter.

FRESH TOMATO SAUCE

MAYONNAISE   ½ cup
LEMON JUICE   2 teaspoons
SALT   ½ teaspoon
INSTANT MINCED ONION   ¼ teaspoon
GARLIC POWDER   ¼ teaspoon
DILL WEED   ⅛ teaspoon
WHITE PEPPER   pinch
TOMATOES   ½ cup peeled and diced

Mix all ingredients but tomatoes in top of double boiler. Cook and stir gently over hot water until heated through. Stir in tomatoes and serve immediately. Makes about 1 cup.

NOTE: The appearance of this sauce may be spoiled by reheating, but the flavor gets even better if it stands a day or so and then is reheated.

PIQUANT PECAN SAUCE

BUTTER   ½ cup, melted
PECANS   3 to 4 tablespoons chopped
LEMON JUICE   1 tablespoon
SALT   ¼ teaspoon
PEPPER   dash

Blend all ingredients, heat gently, and serve with freshly cooked hot asparagus. Makes about ¾ cup.

NOTE: This sauce gets better with time. Make a day ahead and let pecans absorb lemony flavor; reheat gently.

CLAMANDAISE SAUCE

HOLLANDAISE SAUCE (see index)   1 cup*
MINCED or BABY CLAMS   1 cup

Heat hollandaise sauce gently over boiling water. Heat clams in their own juice; drain and save juice for other uses. Purée equal measures of the 2 ingredients together in blender until desired consistency is reached. Keep warm over boiling water until serving time. Makes about 2 cups.

Canned hollandaise sauce may be used instead.

HAM AND HUMMUS SAUCE

HIDDEN VALLEY RANCH SALAD DRESSING   ⅓ cup
HUMMUS   ¾ cup*
ONION   1 tablespoon minced
COOKED HAM   ⅓ cup chopped

Make dressing according to package directions, adding mayonnaise and buttermilk. Mix all ingredients together in blender until smooth. Makes about 1½ cups.

*Hummus can be bought canned, sometimes with tehina (sesame butter) added. The canned product is ideal for this recipe. But since hummus is essentially a garbanzo bean pâté, you can make your own by mixing, preferably with a blender, cooked and mashed garbanzo beans (chick peas), minced onion, olive oil, lemon juice or vinegar, salt, and spices to taste.

Main Dishes

This elegant brunch or supper dish was created by John Simmons of Sebastopol, California.

ASPARAGUS MEXICALI

FRESH ASPARAGUS   1½ bunches
COOKING OIL   2 tablespoons
SHERRY   ½ cup
SWEET BASIL   1 tablespoon
GARLIC POWDER   ½ teaspoon or
     GARLIC CLOVES   3, chopped
DILL WEED   ½ teaspoon
SMALL ONION   1, diced
SMALL FRESH GREEN
     CHILI PEPPERS   2, seeded and minced
TOMATO PASTE   1 cup
CHICKEN STOCK   ½ cup
WHITE PEPPER   ⅛ teaspoon
CUMIN   ¼ teaspoon
CELERY SALT   ¼ teaspoon
GROUND GINGER   ¼ teaspoon
SUGAR   1 teaspoon
LEMON JUICE   from 1 lemon
SHARP CHEDDAR CHEESE   ⅓ pound grated
ENGLISH MUFFINS   6, toasted and buttered or
     FRENCH BREAD   12 slices, toasted and buttered

Discard tough ends of asparagus and French-cut spears into ½-inch segments. If it is late in the season and the asparagus is thick, slice lengthwise before making the French cut. Put oil and half the sherry into a skillet or wok. Add sweet basil, garlic, and dill weed. Combine asparagus, onion, and ¾ of chili peppers in skillet and sauté for about 5 minutes or until asparagus is moderately tender. Set aside. Combine tomato paste and chicken stock in saucepan. Add rest of sherry, white pepper, rest of chili peppers, cumin, celery salt, ginger, sugar, and lemon juice. Simmer for 5 to 10 minutes, stirring often enough to keep it from sticking. Put asparagus into casserole dish, mix in most of the cheese, cover with sauce, sprinkle remaining cheese on top, and bake in moderate oven for 45 minutes. Serve on English muffins. Serves 4 to 6.

P & A CASSEROLE

FRESH ASPARAGUS   1 bunch or equivalent
CHICKEN BROTH   ½ cup
PREPARED HORSERADISH   1 tablespoon
WORCESTERSHIRE SAUCE   1 tablespoon
SALT   3 teaspoons or to taste
BASIL LEAVES   1 teaspoon
FRESH GARLIC   to taste
NARROW EGG NOODLES   6 ounces
MEDIUM ONION   1, chopped
BUTTER or MARGARINE   3 tablespoons
COOKED PORK   3½ cups cut up
RICOTTA CHEESE   1 cup
CREAM OF ASPARAGUS SOUP   1 10½-ounce can
FRESH MUSHROOMS   1 cup sliced
JERUSALEM ARTICHOKE   ¾ cup sliced*
SOURDOUGH FRENCH BREAD CRUMBS   1 cup fine and dry

Cook asparagus until just crunchy-tender; drain thoroughly and cut into bite-size pieces. Put chicken broth into small bowl and add next 5 ingredients. Cook noodles as directed; drain well. Sauté onion in 1 tablespoon of the butter until golden. In large bowl, combine noodles, asparagus, pork, ricotta, soup, onion, mushrooms, and artichoke. Pour in seasoning mix and mix thoroughly; put into large buttered casserole. Melt remaining 2 tablespoons butter and mix with bread crumbs; top casserole with crumbs. Bake at 350° for 1 hour or until crumbs are browned. Serves 6.

*If unavailable, try water chestnuts or celery.

ONIONS DIVAN

AUTUMN'S ASPARAGUS PURÉE (see index)   1 cup
LARGE ONIONS   4
CHICKEN BROTH or BOUILLON
BACON SLICES   4
JICAMA ROOT   ½ cup peeled and diced*
PINE NUTS   to taste
LEMON JUICE   to taste
BUTTER or MARGARINE   to taste
MONTEREY JACK CHEESE   4 small slices
CHEDDAR CHEESE   ½ cup grated
PIMIENTO-STUFFED GREEN OLIVES   garnish

Make purée or remove from refrigerator and let warm. Peel onions; parboil in chicken broth for about 30 minutes or until almost tender. Meanwhile, fry bacon until crisp; drain and crumble. When onions are tender, cut slice from top of each (and from bottom if needed to make them sit well) and hollow out with sharp spoon, leaving as thin a shell as will stand up. Save centers for other uses. Mix purée, jicama pieces, and pine nuts. Brush insides of onion cups with lemon juice and then with butter. Lay cheese slice on bottom of cup and fill each with purée mixture. Top with grated cheese. Press a circle of crumbled bacon into the center of the cheese layer, and garnish each with a slice of olive. Place onions in a pan or baking dish with about ½-inch chicken broth. Bake in a 400° oven until onions are fully tender but still intact and filling is thoroughly heated. Test at 30 minutes. Serves 4.

*Jerusalem artichoke or water chestnuts may be used instead.

HEALTHY ASPARAGUS CASSEROLE

FRESH ASPARAGUS   1½ pounds
BUTTER or MARGARINE   3 tablespoons
FLOUR   2 tablespoons
SALT   ½ teaspoon
WHITE PEPPER   ⅛ teaspoon
MILK   2 cups
YOGURT   ½ cup
ONION JUICE   1 teaspoon
SWISS CHEESE   1 cup grated
BLUE CHEESE   ½ cup crumbled
EGGS   6, hard-cooked
PARSLEY   2 tablespoons minced
WHEAT GERM   ⅔ cup

Cut asparagus into bite-size pieces and cook until crunchy-tender. Melt 2 tablespoons butter; blend in flour, salt, pepper, milk, and yogurt. Cook, stirring, until mixture boils and thickens. Stir in onion juice and cheeses; stir until cheese melts and is well blended. Put half of asparagus in bottom of buttered, shallow 1½-quart baking dish. Melt rest of butter and mash with eggs and parsley in a bowl. Sprinkle asparagus with half the wheat germ and half the egg mixture. Spoon on half the cheese sauce. Arrange rest of asparagus over sauce. Reserve 2 tablespoons wheat germ and sprinkle the rest over the asparagus; then carefully add the rest of the cheese sauce. Arrange rest of egg mixture on top of cheese sauce; sprinkle with remaining wheat germ. Bake in 350° oven for 20 to 25 minutes or until sauce bubbles. Serves 4 to 6.

ASPARAGUS SHORTCAKE

GIANT BISCUITS   6, extra-rich
FRESH ASPARAGUS   1 bunch or equivalent
WINE/CREAM SAUCE (see index)   1½ cups
SWEET BUTTER   2 tablespoons
ANCHOVY PASTE   1 heaping teaspoon
PAPRIKA   garnish

Using your favorite biscuit recipe or mix, prepare 6 biscuits, 4 to 6 inches across. While biscuits bake, cut asparagus into small bite-size pieces and cook until just crunchy-tender; drain and keep hot. Prepare or heat up cream sauce and add asparagus to it. Cream butter and anchovy paste. Cut biscuits in half and spread each with anchovy butter. Pour creamed asparagus over lower half of each biscuit, replace top, and pour more creamed asparagus over all. Dust each with paprika and serve at once. Serves 6.

DOUBLE-OLIVE ASPARAGUS CASSEROLE

FRESH ASPARAGUS   1 bunch
JICAMA ROOT or WATER CHESTNUTS   1 cup diced
EGGS   6, hard-cooked and sliced
SWISS CHEESE   ⅓ cup grated
CHEDDAR CHEESE   ⅓ cup grated
BEER   2 tablespoons
BASIC WHITE SAUCE   2 cups
GREEN OLIVES   6 or to taste, sliced
MONTEREY JACK CHEESE   1 cup grated
BLACK OLIVES   ½ cup sliced
SHRIMP-FLAVORED BREAD CRUMBS (see index)   1 cup

Cut asparagus into bite-size pieces and cook until just crunchy-tender. Drain and spread evenly over bottom of buttered 2-quart baking dish; sprinkle with jicama root. Layer egg slices over asparagus. Prepare cheese sauce by adding Swiss cheese, cheddar cheese, and beer to basic white sauce. Stir in green olive slices and pour over eggs. Top with Monterey jack cheese, black olive slices, and crumbs. Bake at 350° about 20 minutes until crumbs are browned and cheese is bubbling. Serves 4 to 6.

TRIPLE PROTEIN CASSEROLE

FRESH ASPARAGUS   1 bunch
ONION   ¾ cup chopped
BACON DRIPPINGS   4 tablespoons
FLOUR   4 tablespoons
CHICKEN BROTH   ¾ cup
MILK   1 cup
WORCESTERSHIRE SAUCE   1 tablespoon
COOKED HAM   2 cups cut into strips
COOKED CHICKEN   2 cups diced
JICAMA ROOT or WATER CHESTNUTS   1 cup diced
SMALL-CURD COTTAGE CHEESE   1 cup
SOFT BREAD CRUMBS   ½ cup
BUTTER or MARGARINE   2 tablespoons, melted

Cut asparagus into bite-size pieces and cook until just underdone; drain and set aside. Sauté onion in bacon drippings until delicately browned; place in double boiler over boiling water, add flour, and mix well. Add broth, milk, and Worcestershire sauce and cook until thickened, stirring occasionally. Cover and cook 15 minutes. While sauce is in last cooking period, arrange ham, asparagus, chicken, jicama root, and cottage cheese in that order in 2-quart casserole. Pour sauce over all. Top with crumbs mixed with butter and bake at 375° for 30 minutes. Serves 6 to 8.

Only Chinese cooks seem to be brave enough to make asparagus and beef a usual combination. This recipe combines Chinese and Hawaiian inspirations.

ASPARAGUS STIR-FRY MARINATED BEEF

VERY TENDER BEEF   1 pound
MILD VINEGAR   ¼ cup
SOY SAUCE   4 teaspoons
OYSTER SAUCE   4 teaspoons
DRY SHERRY   6 teaspoons
SALAD OIL   2 teaspoons
SESAME SEED OIL   1 teaspoon
SUGAR   1 teaspoon
WHITE PEPPER   dash
MSG   dash
FRESH ASPARAGUS   2 pounds
SALAD OIL   ¼ cup plus 3 tablespoons
MEDIUM ONION   1, coarsely chopped
WATER CHESTNUTS   1 6½-ounce can, drained and sliced
SALT   1 teaspoon
SUGAR   ½ teaspoon
SOY SAUCE   1 tablespoon
RICE   4 to 5 servings
SESAME SEEDS   ¼ cup, lightly toasted

If in doubt about meat's tenderness, pound it or use tenderizer. Cut meat into bite-size pieces about 1½ inches long, ½ inch wide, and ¼ to ⅛ inch thick. Mix next 9 ingredients to make marinade and put in container big enough to hold meat as well. Cover and refrigerate for 4 hours. Stir occasionally or, if the container's lid is tight enough, just turn the whole thing over from time to time. *Just before serving,* remove meat from marinade and drain on paper towel. Slice tender parts of asparagus diagonally into pieces about ¼ inch thick. The Oriental secret here is to slice on a sharp diagonal so that the pieces are attractive ovals, 1½ to 2 inches long. Put ¼ cup salad oil in skillet or wok over high heat. When oil bubbles, add meat and stir-fry until almost browned; remove to warm place. Add 3 tablespoons more oil and put in onion and water chestnuts. Cook, stirring, until onion begins to get translucent; then stir in asparagus. Sprinkle with salt, sugar, and soy sauce, and mix in thoroughly. Cover and cook, stirring occasionally, just until asparagus is tender-crisp. Put meat back in, and stir-cook just long enough to reheat. Serve at once over rice and garnish with sesame seeds. Serves 4 to 5.

VARIETY ROLLUPS

FRESH ASPARAGUS   1 pound or
    FROZEN ASPARAGUS   1 10-ounce package
CREAM CHEESE   4-ounce package, softened
MAYONNAISE   2 tablespoons
DILL WEED   1 teaspoon
DELICATESSEN-STYLE
    BREAST OF TURKEY   1 package or 6 thin slices
GREY POUPON MUSTARD   to taste
HAM or PROSCIUTTO   1 package or 6 thin slices
MONTEREY JACK CHEESE   6 slices,
    ¾-inch wide and asparagus length

Briefly parboil fresh asparagus or thaw frozen asparagus. Drain and divide spears into 9 piles of 2 to 4 spears each (fat asparagus will have about 24 spears; slender asparagus, about 36). Mix cream cheese, mayonnaise, and dill weed, and spread on turkey slices. Lightly spread mustard on ham slices. Put a Monterey jack slice with 6 of the 9 piles. Roll the 3 plain asparagus piles in 3 of the spread turkey slices; secure with toothpick and set aside. Roll 3 of the cheese-and-asparagus piles in 3 of the ham slices; secure and set aside. Roll remaining 3 piles in *both* turkey and ham slices, ham outside. Secure and set aside. Alternate varieties of rollups in 8 x 8-inch baking dish. Pour Wine/Cream Sauce over rollups. Bake at 375° for 20 to 25 minutes. Serves 3 to 4.

WINE/CREAM SAUCE

WHITE WINE ⅓ cup
WHOLE MILK 1⅔ cups
FLOUR 4½ tablespoons
BUTTER or MARGARINE 3 tablespoons, melted
SALT ½ teaspoon
CAYENNE dash
HEAVY CREAM or EVAPORATED MILK 1 tablespoon

To hot wine-milk mixture, add paste made of flour, butter, and seasonings. Cook over low heat, whisking constantly. When mixture thickens, stir in cream. Pour over rollups in baking dish. There should be enough to cover generously and still have leftover sauce for another dish later.

ASPARAGUS SUNRISE CORNBREAD

AUTUMN'S ASPARAGUS PURÉE (see index)   ½ cup
DRY MUSTARD   ½ teaspoon
CORNBREAD MIX   1 15-ounce package
COOKED HAM   4 thin slices*
CHEDDAR CHEESE   1 cup grated
EGGS   4, besides egg needed for mix

Make purée and add dry mustard. (If you use canned asparagus, add ¼ teaspoon sugar.) Prepare cornbread mix as directed or make your own batter. Grease 8- or 9-inch square glass pan and pour in enough batter to cover the bottom. Bake 3 to 4 minutes (less for larger pan) at temperature called for by package directions. Meanwhile, spread purée on ham slices and sprinkle ¾ of the cheese over the purée. Remove cornbread from oven, quickly lay the ham slices on top of the partly baked batter, without overlapping, and then pour on remaining batter. Sprinkle remaining cheese on top and put back in oven for the rest of the baking time, taking particular care not to overbake. Just before cornbread is to come out, fry eggs sunny side up, and serve one on top of each serving of cornbread. With a tossed green salad or homemade coleslaw, this makes a fine weekend supper. Serves 4.

*Chopped leftover ham or chipped beef can also be used here, in which case the asparagus purée is merely dotted over the meat; or finely chopped cooked asparagus can be used instead of purée. If using chipped beef, change cheese to cream cheese.

ASPARAGUS AND DILLY EGGS IN A NOODLE NEST

FRESH ASPARAGUS   2 pounds
DRIED BEEF   1 5-ounce jar
FLOUR   ¼ cup
BUTTER or MARGARINE   ¼ cup
MILK   1 cup
CHICKEN BROTH   1 cup
CHIVES   1 tablespoon snipped
SALT   1 teaspoon
DILL WEED   ½ teaspoon
EGGS   6, hard-cooked and sliced
CHIPPED BEEF   garnish
CHOW MEIN NOODLES   2 5-ounce cans*

Cook asparagus until crunchy-tender; keep warm. Chop cut dried beef into slivers; set aside. Make a paste of flour and butter in saucepan; remove from heat and stir in milk, chicken broth, and seasonings. Return to heat and cook until moderately thick. Add egg slices, mixing lightly to keep slices intact. On serving platter, mound asparagus spears in center, cover with creamed eggs, and garnish with chipped beef. Surround with crisp chow mein noodles to form a nest. Serves 6.

*If these Chinese noodles are not available in your area, use canned shoestring potatoes.

LAMB ARGENTEUIL

FRESH ASPARAGUS   3 bunches or
    FROZEN ASPARAGUS   4 10-ounce packages
AUTUMN'S ASPARAGUS PURÉE (see index)   ½ recipe
SMALL LEG OF LAMB   1, boned and cut in 1-inch pieces
ONIONS   2 large or 4 small, coarsely chopped (about 2 cups)
BUTTER or MARGARINE   4 tablespoons
FRESH MUSHROOMS   1 cup sliced
FLOUR   1½ tablespoons
SOUR CREAM   ½ cup
LEMON JUICE   to taste
CURRY POWDER   dash
SALT   to taste
RICE   8 servings

Take tops of 1 bunch of asparagus and make half a recipe of Autumn's Asparagus Purée. Steam other 2 bunches until underdone in about 1 inch of water. Drain, and save the water. Cut spears into 1½- to 2-inch pieces and keep warm. Meanwhile, brown lamb and onions lightly in butter. Add mushrooms. Stir in flour and about 1 cup of the asparagus water, and cook gently until meat is done, stirring occasionally. Be sure liquid evaporates slowly. Adjust consistency of sauce by adding more flour or more asparagus cooking liquid, as necessary. When lamb is done, stir in sour cream and heat gently until things begin to thicken. Add asparagus purée and bring back to boil. Add cut-up asparagus and just heat through. Put in lemon juice until flavor is as sharp as you like it; add curry powder, and salt as needed. The sauce should be a lovely and unusual green, well blended, and substantial without being heavy. Serve at once over rice. Serves 8.

SPARROWGRASS TIMBALES

BUTTER or MARGARINE   melted
FRESH SLENDER ASPARAGUS   1 bunch
COOKED HAM   4 thin slices
LARGE EGGS   3, well beaten
MILK   1¾ cups warm
SALT   ½ teaspoon
ONION SALT   ¾ teaspoon
NUTMEG   ¼ teaspoon
FRESH LEMON JUICE   1 teaspoon
MONTEREY JACK CHEESE   ½ cup grated
WINE/CREAM SAUCE (see index)
DRY MUSTARD   1 teaspoon
FRESH SPINACH   1 cup chopped

Generously butter 4 custard cups. Trim asparagus spears so they stand on bottom of custard cups and tips come just above rim; *briefly* parboil and drain. Line custard cups with ham slices, trimming and slitting as necessary. Mix eggs, milk, salt, onion salt, nutmeg, lemon juice, and cheese. Stand asparagus spears around edges of cups. Carefully pour egg mixture into cups so that spears remain standing; brush tips with melted butter both now and as needed during baking. Set cups in a pan of hot water and bake at 325° for 1¼ hours or until a knife inserted into center of custard comes out clean. Turn out on plates and serve with Wine/Cream Sauce to which mustard has been added. Garnish with spinach. Serves 4.

SPARROWGRASS AND SAUSAGE PIZZA

Make enough dough for a large pizza (the large size served in most pizza parlors), using your own favorite recipe or mix, or using 4 parts Bisquick Buttermilk Baking Mix and 1 part milk. Roll out and place on pizza pan or greased cookie sheet, making a rim of dough around edges. Make topping as follows:

MOZZARELLA CHEESE   about 16 slices or
    8 ounces or as needed
MILD COUNTRY-STYLE PORK SAUSAGE   1 pound
SWEET BASIL   ¼ teaspoon
OREGANO   ¼ teaspoon
WHITE CLAM SAUCE   1 6-ounce can (Buitoni)*
CORNSTARCH   up to 5 teaspoons
RAW ASPARAGUS TIPS   1 cup
MUSHROOMS   1 4-ounce can sliced
FRESH TOMATO   12 thin slices
PARMESAN CHEESE   to taste, grated

Lay mozzarella slices directly on dough, arranging them evenly and preferably covering entire surface. Add more slices if needed. Brown sausage gently and pour off drippings; crumble. Add basil and oregano to clam sauce, and heat gently with cornstarch as needed to thicken. Pour thickened sauce over cheese slices. Sprinkle sausage, asparagus tips, and mushrooms evenly over surface of pizza; arrange tomato slices on top. Sprinkle all with Parmesan to taste. Bake at 400° for 15 to 20 minutes or until done. Serves 4.

If you cannot buy white clam sauce in your area, you can make your own with minced clams, butter, white wine, and Italian-style seasonings to taste.

SAUSAGE AND ASPARAGUS SUPPER

MILD COUNTRY-STYLE SAUSAGE   2 pounds
FRESH ASPARAGUS   1 small bunch
CONDENSED CREAM OF MUSHROOM SOUP   1 10½-ounce can
FRESH MUSHROOMS   ½ cup chopped
SHARP CHEDDAR CHEESE   ¾ cup grated
ASPARAGUS-FLAVORED NOODLES   4 servings*
BUTTERED BREAD CRUMBS   1 cup

Brown sausage gently and pour off drippings. Crumble. Keep hot. Cut asparagus into bite-size pieces; cook until crunchy-tender; drain, reserving ½ cup of liquid. Keep asparagus hot. Mix soup, mushrooms, asparagus liquid, and cheese in saucepan; cook over low heat until well mixed and thick. Keep hot. Prepare noodles according to package directions; drain and pour into buttered casserole dish. Add sausage, asparagus, and cheese sauce, in that order. Top with bread crumbs and place in hot oven (425°) just long enough to brown crumbs. Serves 4.

*If not available, use spinach noodles or ordinary noodles.

VEAL SOMEWHAT A LA OSCAR

FRESH ASPARAGUS   1 bunch
WINE/CREAM SAUCE (see index)   1 cup
WINE VINEGAR   4½ tablespoons
PREPARED HORSERADISH   1 teaspoon
ONION   2 tablespoons minced
EGG YOLKS   2
BUTTER   6 tablespoons
TENDER BONELESS VEAL   6 slices
BUTTER   2 to 3 tablespoons
SALT   1½ teaspoons
CRAB MEAT   6 ounces flaked and warmed
PARSLEY   garnish
RICE or NOODLES   6 servings

Cook asparagus until fork-tender; drain. Reserve 2 to 3 spears for top of each veal slice; cut rest into small bite-size pieces and set aside. Make cream sauce and stir in cut-up asparagus; keep hot. To make egg sauce, heat vinegar and seasonings; add 1 egg yolk and beat well; add half the butter and beat well; repeat. Pound veal if it is not tender; sauté in butter, salting it as it cooks for 2 to 3 minutes. Add veal juice from pan to egg sauce, beating vigorously. Fold in crab meat. Arrange veal slices on hot serving platter with asparagus spears on top. Pour cream sauce over meat and asparagus; then top with egg sauce/crab mixture. Bring any extra sauce to table. Garnish with parsley and serve at once with rice or noodles. Serves 6.

ASPARAGUS LOAF WITH SWEETBREADS

FRESH ASPARAGUS   1 pound
CONDENSED CREAM OF ASPARAGUS SOUP   1 10½-ounce can
RICH MILK   1¼ cups
ONION   1 tablespoon minced
GARLIC CLOVE   ½, minced
NUTMEG   dash
EGG YOLKS   6
SALT and WHITE PEPPER   to taste
PIMIENTOS   1 4½-ounce jar, cut into strips
COOKED SWEETBREADS   1 cup chopped
ENDIVE or PARSLEY   garnish
CHERRY TOMATOES   garnish
SOUR CREAM   1 pint

Cook asparagus until crunchy-tender and drain. Combine soup and milk; add onion, garlic, and nutmeg. Beat in egg yolks already seasoned with salt and pepper. Arrange asparagus spears and pimiento strips in pleasing pattern on bottom of buttered 11 x 7-inch glass baking dish. (The pattern will be on top when loaf is turned out.) Arrange sweetbreads evenly over asparagus. Pour egg mixture over all. Set baking dish in pan of hot water and bake at 350° for about 40 minutes or until set (when pick or knife inserted into center comes out clean). When done, loosen edges with knife and turn out onto platter. Garnish with endive and tomatoes. Heat sour cream gently and offer as accompanying sauce for the loaf. Serves 4 to 6.

This mouth-watering dish was created by Susan Eastwood of Burlingame, California.

SPARROWGRASS CHICKEN

CHICKEN   3 pounds, cut up, or 1 breast per serving
FRESH or FROZEN ASPARAGUS   2 pounds or equivalent
WHITE or LIGHT RED WINE or CHAMPAGNE   ¼ cup
CREAM OF ASPARAGUS SOUP   2 10½-ounce cans
SOUR CREAM   1 pint
LEMON JUICE   1 teaspoon
TABASCO SAUCE   2 dashes
THYME   2 pinches
MUSHROOMS   ½ pound, sliced
SWISS CHEESE   ½ pound, grated
PAPRIKA   garnish
RICE   8 servings

Bone chicken pieces and remove skin. Steam asparagus until crunchy-tender. Reserve 3 to 4 spears for garnish. Meanwhile, heat a heavy skillet or pot until water skitters on it, and braise the chicken pieces in the pot, turning with a wooden spoon until cooked. Remove chicken and keep warm. Turn heat to low. Pour wine into pot and heat gently, loosening braised chicken threads until gravy is formed. Add asparagus soup, sour cream, lemon juice, tabasco, and thyme and stir all together; heat and stir constantly until the first bubble breaks the surface. Remove from heat. Layer sauce, chicken, mushrooms, asparagus, and cheese, in that order, in an ovenproof casserole dish or serving pot. End with a layer of sauce. Top with asparagus spears and sprinkle all with paprika. Heat at 350° in covered casserole for about 30 minutes or until warmed through. Serve over rice. Serves 8.

CHICKEN PELLAO WITH ASPARAGUS

FRESH ASPARAGUS   ½ pound
RICE   1 pound
CHICKEN BROTH
BUTTER or MARGARINE   3 tablespoons
CARDAMOM SEEDS   4
PEPPERCORNS   2, crushed
COOKED CHICKEN   2 cups boned and shredded
HEAVY CREAM   ½ cup
CORIANDER   ½ tablespoon
SALT   to taste

Cook asparagus stalks until barely tender; save liquor. Boil rice in all but ¼ cup of asparagus liquor, adding chicken broth if necessary to make enough liquid. In skillet, melt butter and fry cardamom seeds and peppercorns. Add asparagus and lightly fry for no more than 5 minutes. Place seasoned asparagus in casserole; add ¼ cup asparagus liquor, then rice, then a layer of chicken. Pour cream over this and sprinkle with coriander and salt to taste. Mix well but gently. Cover tightly and cook over brisk heat for 5 minutes. Put in preheated 250° oven and bake for 20 minutes. Serves 6.

NOTE: For a vegetarian dish, simply omit the chicken and use water instead of chicken broth for extra rice cooking liquid.

CHICKEN, SAN JUAN STYLE

MEDIUM ONION   1, chopped
BUTTER or MARGARINE   3 tablespoons
FRYER   1, cut up
SALT   to taste
RICE   1 cup
SAFFRON   pinch
PIMIENTOS   ½ cup cut up
FROZEN ASPARAGUS   1 10-ounce package
FROZEN PEAS   1 10-ounce package
PITTED GREEN OLIVES   1 small jar
CHICKEN BROTH   2 cups
DRY WHITE WINE   1 cup
LEMON JUICE   1 tablespoon

Sauté onion in butter until golden. Add chicken pieces and brown on both sides, adding salt to taste. Cook rice with saffron until it is done as you like it. Transfer chicken and onions to deep casserole dish; add rice, pimientos, asparagus, peas, and olives. Sprinkle asparagus and peas with salt. Mix broth, wine, and lemon juice and pour over all. Cover and bake at 300° for about 45 minutes or until chicken is tender. Serve with French bread, candied orange peel, and cream cheese. Serves 4 to 6.

EGGS A L'OPÉRA AUTOMNE

CHICKEN GIZZARDS   6
SALT   to taste
FRESH ASPARAGUS   1 bunch
CHICKEN LIVERS   12 to 16
BUTTER or MARGARINE
ONION SALT   to taste
EGGS   6 to 8
LEMON JUICE   1 teaspoon
PREPARED HORSERADISH   ½ teaspoon
VEAL GRAVY   1 cup*

Boil gizzards in salted water for about 45 minutes until very tender. Cut up and purée in blender with enough of their own broth to keep mixture moist. Save rest of broth for other uses. Cook well-trimmed asparagus until fork-tender. Meanwhile, cook chicken livers until underdone in butter; season with onion salt. Butter a shallow baking dish, and cover the bottom with drained asparagus. Break eggs over asparagus so as to create distinct servings; salt to taste and flank each egg with 2 chicken livers. In a preheated 350° oven, cook for 8 to 12 minutes or until eggs are done as you like them. Add lemon juice, horseradish, and gizzard purée to veal gravy; heat. Spoon over eggs and asparagus just before serving. Serves 6 to 8.

*If you have no veal gravy, use half beef and half chicken broth or bouillon thickened with flour and cream.

BREAST OF CHICKEN PALATINA

CHICKEN BREASTS   4, boned and dredged
   in flour, paprika, and salt
BUTTER or MARGARINE   5½ tablespoons
CARROTS   1 cup baby or sliced
FROZEN or FRESH PEAS
   ½ 10-ounce package or fresh equivalent
FRESH ASPARAGUS   tips from 1 to 2 bunches
LARGE EGGPLANT   1
FLOUR
COOKING OIL   several tablespoons
DANISH-STYLE COOKED HAM   4 slices
EGG   1, lightly beaten
PARMESAN CHEESE   3 ounces, grated
FRESH MUSHROOMS   1 cup sliced
CREAM   ½ cup
MADEIRA or DRY SHERRY   ½ cup

Using a deep skillet, brown chicken quickly in 3 tablespoons of the butter and cook slowly until tender and golden brown. Add a little cooking oil if necessary. Meanwhile, cook carrots (if necessary) until tender; add peas at the end, being careful not to overcook. Keep warm. Steam asparagus tips about 2 minutes or leave raw if you like that texture. If cooked, keep warm. Make 4 thin slices from large end of eggplant, coat with flour, and fry in cooking oil until barely done (if overdone, they will fall apart). Keep warm. Wrap ham slices tightly in foil and warm in oven. Make a paste of 1½ tablespoons melted butter, lightly beaten egg, and cheese. Set aside. When chicken is done, remove from skillet and keep hot in oven. Put mushrooms into chicken pan and sauté briefly; then add cream and Madeira and boil about 1 minute. Make a paste of 1 tablespoon flour and 1 tablespoon butter in small pan. Cook about 3 minutes, stirring often. Add half the mushroom-cream-Madeira sauce, blend with a whisk, and cook until thickened. Set aside, but keep hot. Turn heat to very low under chicken skillet. Lay ham slices in remaining unthickened sauce; do not overlap.

Spread eggplant slices with cheese mixture and lay one on each ham slice. Put chicken breasts on eggplant slices. Surround chicken with asparagus, carrots, and peas. Pour thickened sauce from small pan over all. Cover, heat through, and serve immediately. Serves 4.

TURKEY DIVAN

FRESH ASPARAGUS   1 bunch
BUTTER   1 tablespoon, melted
ROMANO CHEESE   3 tablespoons grated
MADEIRA   6 tablespoons
COOKED TURKEY   2 cups flaked
BEAN SPROUTS   1 cup
WINE/CREAM SAUCE (see index)   1 cup
EGG YOLKS   2, slightly beaten
GARLIC POWDER   to taste
SOUR CREAM   2 tablespoons

Butter a shallow baking dish; in bottom, lay asparagus spears, cooked until just fork-tender. Sprinkle with melted butter, 1 tablespoon Romano cheese, and 2 tablespoons Madeira. Spread turkey and bean sprouts over seasoned asparagus, and sprinkle again with 1 tablespoon Romano and 2 tablespoons Madeira. Into Wine/Cream Sauce, stir egg yolks and add garlic powder to taste. Fold in the sour cream and pour over turkey layer. Sprinkle for the third time with 1 tablespoon Romano and 2 tablespoons Madeira. Bake at 350° for about 12 minutes or until delicately browned. Serves 4.

SNOW-TOPPED ASPARAGUS

FRESH, FROZEN, or CANNED
    CRAB MEAT   ½ pound cooked and flaked
LEMON JUICE   to taste
FRESH or FROZEN ASPARAGUS   1 bunch or equivalent*
GREEN ONION   2 tablespoons sliced
BUTTER or MARGARINE   2 tablespoons
FLOUR   1 tablespoon
SALT   ¾ teaspoon
PREPARED HORSERADISH   1 teaspoon
GARLIC POWDER   dash
HALF-AND-HALF   1 cup
CHIVES   1 tablespoon finely chopped
WATER CHESTNUTS   ¼ cup chopped
KRAFT SALAD DRESSING   ⅓ cup (not mayonnaise)
SHRIMP-FLAVORED BREAD CRUMBS (see index)   2 tablespoons
PARMESAN CHEESE   1½ tablespoons grated
PAPRIKA   garnish

If crab meat is frozen, thaw in advance. Drain, flake, and sprinkle with lemon juice. Cook asparagus until fork-tender; drain and keep warm on heatproof platter. Cook green onion in butter until golden; stir in flour, salt, horseradish, and garlic. Add half-and-half and cook, stirring, until thick. Remove from heat and stir in chives, water chestnuts, and salad dressing. Add crab and heat through. Arrange asparagus spears on heatproof oval platter or shallow baking dish so that tips point toward both ends of platter and ends meet or overlap in center. Spoon crab sauce over asparagus, not covering tips. Sprinkle with bread crumbs, cheese, and paprika. Put under broiler, about 4 inches from heat, just until lightly browned and heated through (about 3 to 5 minutes). Serves 4.

Since serving will be awkward if asparagus does not cut easily, use only tender ends of asparagus or peel bottoms of spears.

PERCH JULIETTE WITH AVOCADO

PERCH or BUTTERFISH FILLETS   4
WHITE WINE   enough for poaching
LEMON JUICE   ¼ cup
SALT and PEPPER   to taste
WHITE ASPARAGUS SPEARS   1 15½-ounce can
RIPE AVOCADO   1, sliced
SMOKED SALMON   3 ounces
CAPERS   2 tablespoons
CELERY   ½ cup finely chopped
UNFLAVORED GELATIN   3 envelopes
WHITE WINE   1 tablespoon
CREAM CHEESE SAUCE #2 (see index)

Poach fish in wine to which 2 tablespoons of the lemon juice, and salt and pepper, have been added. Drain, reserving ¼ cup of liquid. Arrange drained fillets, asparagus spears, and avocado slices in bottom of shallow serving dish. Decorate with salmon strips and capers. Fill any remaining spaces on bottom of dish with celery. Mix gelatin and cold water as in package directions. Add ¼ cup of fish poaching liquid, remaining lemon juice, and 1 tablespoon more white wine to hot water to make up the total of hot liquid needed to finish dissolving gelatin (fish should be *nearly* covered); heat until fully dissolved. Pour carefully over fish. Chill until set, and serve with Cream Cheese Sauce #2. Serves 4.

SHRIMP FRIES ASPARAGUS

FRESH SHRIMP   1 pound peeled
SMALL ONION   1, coarsely cut
COOKING OIL   2 tablespoons
FRESH ASPARAGUS   1 bunch
GARLIC JUICE   ½ teaspoon
SUGAR   1 teaspoon
GROUND GINGER   ½ teaspoon
SOY SAUCE   2 tablespoons
LEMON JUICE   1 tablespoon
SESAME SEEDS   2 tablespoons
RICE   4 servings

If shrimp are large, cut into ½-inch pieces; sauté with onion in hot oil until shrimp turn pink. Slice asparagus on very thin diagonals and add to skillet with next 5 ingredients. Cook 3 to 5 minutes or until shrimp are tender, using high heat and stirring constantly at first, then covering to steam for last minute or two. Sprinkle with sesame seeds. Serve hot with rice. Serves 4.

ASPARAGUS-STUFFED SQUASH

LARGE BUTTERNUT SQUASH   1
CHICKEN BROTH or BOUILLON   salted
SHRIMP   1 4½-ounce can
STALE SOURDOUGH FRENCH BREAD   3 slices
BUTTER or MARGARINE
JERUSALEM ARTICHOKE or WATER CHESTNUTS   1 or equivalent
LEMON JUICE   to taste
MONTEREY JACK CHEESE   1 cup grated
SALT   to taste
AUTUMN'S ASPARAGUS PURÉE (see index)   1 cup
BLACK OLIVES   1 cup sliced
CHEDDAR CHEESE   1 cup grated

Scrub squash, cut in half lengthwise, and hollow out both natural cavity and neck; lay halves cut side down in ½-inch chicken broth in shallow pan, and bake until nearly tender (*at least* 1 to 1¼ hours). While squash is prebaking, prepare stuffing. Drain shrimp and reserve liquid; set drained shrimp aside. Soak stale French bread in shrimp liquid; spread with butter and toast dry in oven. Break toast into 1- to 2-inch pieces and reduce to crumbs in blender. This should make about ½ cup of shrimp-flavored bread crumbs. (These flavored crumbs can be used in many dishes. Eight to ten slices of a medium-size loaf will make about 2 cups of fine crumbs.) Scrub artichoke thoroughly and peel; slice fairly thin and quarter the slices. When prebaking time is over, remove squash from oven and turn cut side up in pan. Brush cavities with butter, and squeeze lemon juice liberally into them. Into each squash half, put a layer of Monterey jack cheese, artichoke slices sprinkled with salt (this layer should generally be only 1 slice thick), asparagus purée, olives, shrimp, cheddar cheese, and finally the bread crumbs. Bake at 375° for 30 to 60 minutes or until squash cases are tender and filling is thoroughly heated. Test with a toothpick after 30 minutes. Serves 6 to 8.

NOTE: The color combination here with the green, black, and pale yellow of the filling and the rich golden orange of the butternut squash is especially nice; but this stuffing can be used for any winter squash or even a big zucchini, with baking times adjusted accordingly. It can also be layered in eggplant and zucchini casseroles.

FILLET OF SOLE DIVAN

LONG GRAIN RICE   1 cup
FRESH ASPARAGUS   1½ pounds or
      FROZEN ASPARAGUS   1 10-ounce package
CELERY   1 cup finely chopped
BUTTER or MARGARINE   3 tablespoons
FLOUR   3 tablespoons
MILK   1 cup
SALT   1 teaspoon
WORCESTERSHIRE SAUCE   1 teaspoon
PREPARED HORSERADISH   1 tablespoon
FRESH LEMON JUICE   2 tablespoons
WATER CHESTNUTS   ½ cup diced
SOUR CREAM   1 cup
LEMON JUICE   from ½ lemon
SOLE FILLETS   8 or about 2 pounds
ROMANO CHEESE   2 tablespoons grated
ALMONDS   3 tablespoons sliced and toasted

Cook rice as directed and put in bottom of buttered 11 x 7 x 2-inch glass baking dish. Cook well-trimmed asparagus until just crunchy-tender and drain. Sauté celery in butter until it begins to get translucent; stir in flour and cook just 1 minute. Add milk; cook and stir until sauce thickens. Stir in next 5 ingredients. Have sour cream at room temperature; gradually add sauce to it, stirring constantly. Squeeze lemon juice liberally over fillets; salt to taste and roll each fillet around 2 to 3 asparagus spears. Arrange rollups on rice; secure with toothpick if necessary. Pour cream sauce over rollups; sprinkle with cheese and almonds. Bake 25 minutes at 350°. Serves 8.

Omelettes, Soufflés, Quiches, and Crêpes

OMELETTES

There are probably as many different omelettes as there are serious cooks in the world. Some people do not dilute the eggs at all; others use a little water, milk, or cream; I prefer mayonnaise, yogurt, or sour cream, depending partly on what filling I intend to put in the omelette. Some cooks want the skillet very hot and fast. Others want to cook the eggs as slowly and gently as possible.

But there are a few things everyone agrees on: 1) the more you beat the eggs before cooking, the fluffier your omelette; 2) eggs must never brown, for they then take on a most disagreeable flavor; and 3) the fewer eggs you use, the easier the omelette is to handle. On the last point, you will probably find it easier to make individual omelettes for everyone. Large supper omelettes, like the frittata, have to finish cooking in the oven.

All omelettes are subject to variation, and the asparagus omelettes are no exception. Try the following basic recipe.

BASIC ASPARAGUS OMELETTE

EGGS   3
SALT   ¼ teaspoon
WATER   1 tablespoon cold
BUTTER or MARGARINE   1 tablespoon
ASPARAGUS   ⅔ cup cooked and diced
HOLLANDAISE SAUCE (see index)

With wire whisk or rotary beater, beat eggs with salt and water until well mixed. Slowly heat a 9-inch heavy skillet or omelette pan until water dropped on it sizzles and rolls off in drops; put in butter, being careful it does not brown. Pour egg mixture quickly into skillet and cook over medium heat, lifting occasionally with spatula to let uncooked parts run underneath. When partly set, pour on asparagus mixed with hollandaise sauce. Fold over, allow to complete setting, and turn out onto warmed plate. Serve at once with extra sauce. Serves 1 to 2.

VARIATIONS: Add grated cheddar, Swiss, or Monterey jack cheese (or your own favorites), shredded ham, chipped beef and cream cheese, shrimp, crumbled bacon, mushrooms, chicken, chicken livers, or sweetbreads. You might also want to try warmed asparagus purée or one of the other sauces served with hot asparagus, or marinate the asparagus spears in Russian dressing overnight before using them in the omelette.

ASPARAGUS AND GREEN TOMATO OMELETTE

FRESH ASPARAGUS SPEARS   3
ONION   1 tablespoon minced
GREEN TOMATOES   3 plum-size or equivalent, sliced
BUTTER or MARGARINE   melted
EGGS   2
YOGURT   2 heaping teaspoons
SALT   to taste
MONTEREY JACK CHEESE   ¼ cup grated
SOURDOUGH FRENCH BREAD   1 slice, toasted

Slice asparagus spears thin on sharp diagonal. Combine with onion and green tomato slices in melted butter. Sauté briefly until onion is golden and asparagus crunchy-tender. Break eggs into small bowl; add yogurt and salt, and beat until light and frothy. Pour into melted butter in clean skillet that is just hot enough to start the eggs setting. When about half set, add asparagus mixture, and sprinkle with cheese. Continue cooking very slowly until more nearly set, and then fold over. Cook only until cheese is thoroughly melted, and then turn out on plate, never allowing eggs to form a brown skin. Serve at once with sourdough French bread toast. Serves 1.

ASPARAGUS OMELETTE WITH CRAB

FRESH ASPARAGUS SPEARS   8
BUTTER or MARGARINE   3 tablespoons
SMALL ONION   1, minced
SALT   to taste
EGGS   5
SALT   ¼ teaspoon
YOGURT   2 tablespoons
CRAB MEAT   ¼ cup flaked
GRUYÈRE CHEESE   ¼ cup grated*
PARMESAN CHEESE   ¼ cup grated

Slice tender ends of asparagus spears diagonally into very thin slices. Heat butter in 10-inch omelette pan or skillet; add asparagus slices and onion, and cook until asparagus is crunchy-tender and onion is golden and soft; sprinkle lightly with salt. Beat eggs with ¼ teaspoon salt, and yogurt. Pour half of this mixture over asparagus and onion and continue to cook gently, lifting up as egg firms to let uncooked parts run under. Add remaining egg mixture. Sprinkle crab evenly over all, and sprinkle cheese over crab. Cook only until golden brown on bottom but still moist in center. Sprinkle with Parmesan and place under broiler (about 4 inches from heat) until top is well set and golden. Serve at once. Serves 4.

*Use Swiss if you cannot find Gruyère.

This family-style omelette was modified by Nancy Yerby from a Genovese recipe given her by Carolina Ravano. It is served at the New Varsity Restaurant in Palo Alto, California.

FRITTATA RAVANO

SMALL or MEDIUM ONIONS   5, chopped
BUTTER   4 tablespoons
ASPARAGUS SPEARS   20, cut small
SALT and PEPPER   to taste
BREAD   6 slices
MILK   1 cup
EGGS   12
COOKING OIL

Sauté onions in butter until golden; add cut-up asparagus and cook about 5 minutes, seasoning to taste with salt and pepper. Cut crusts off bread; break slices into pieces and soak in milk. Beat eggs well. Drain bread slightly and mix all ingredients together. Coat a hot 12-inch skillet well on bottom and sides with cooking oil, leaving a generous coating of oil on bottom. Pour mixture into pan and brown on one side for about 5 minutes. Put in 350° oven and bake for 30 to 45 minutes or until firm; test with a knife inserted into top. Cut into wedges like pie for serving; wedges will be very thick. Serves 8 to 10.

Soufflés intimidate many cooks—including me. But once you learn the general principle, you can stop being scared: vegetable soufflés are essentially a vegetable purée that is seasoned, lightened with egg, and baked. The only other thing to remember is never to open the oven door to look at the soufflé while it is baking. And soufflés *do* need a preheated oven. Here is a good basic asparagus soufflé to start with.

SPARROWGRASS SOUFFLÉ

AUTUMN'S ASPARAGUS PURÉE (see index)   1½ cups
BUTTER or MARGARINE
DRY MONTEREY JACK CHEESE   grated, to taste
EGG YOLKS   6
SALT   to taste
LEMON PEPPER   to taste*
EGG WHITES   7

Make purée and let it cool. Meanwhile, preheat oven to 325°. Butter the inside of a 2-quart soufflé dish; dust with grated cheese. Beat yolks into cooled purée; mix thoroughly and season with salt and lemon pepper to taste. Beat egg whites until stiff but not dry. Stir in enough of the beaten whites to lighten the asparagus mixture; then carefully *fold in* the rest. Pour mixture into soufflé dish, lightly level the top, and bake at once on the lowest oven shelf for about 40 minutes. If you have a glass door on your oven, you can tell when the soufflé is done: it will be golden brown on top, fully risen, and beginning to pull away from the sides of the dish. Serve at once. Serves 6.

*If lemon pepper is not available in your area, add a little grated lemon rind to regular pepper.

This special soufflé was created by Andrew Griscom and Susan MacDonald of Menlo Park, California.

ASPARAGUS FEAST SOUFFLÉ

FLOUR   4 tablespoons
BUTTER   4 tablespoons
MILK   1½ cups, heated
MUSHROOMS   ½ cup minced
BUTTER   2 tablespoons
GARLIC CLOVE   1, fresh-squeezed
ASPARAGUS   1 cup finely chopped and cooked or
      AUTUMN'S ASPARAGUS PURÉE (see index)   1 cup
SWISS CHEESE   ½ cup grated
SALT and WHITE PEPPER   to taste
SWEET BASIL   big pinch
EGGS   4, separated

Make paste of flour and butter in saucepan. Make a white sauce by adding milk and cooking mixture until smooth and thick; remove from heat. In another pan, sauté the mushrooms in butter flavored with garlic; add mushrooms to white sauce. Add asparagus and cheese to white sauce and cook over low heat until cheese melts. Season to taste with salt, pepper, and basil. Heat oven to 375°. Beat in 4 egg yolks, one at a time; cool mixture. Beat whites until stiff and then fold into cheese mixture; pour into greased 2-quart soufflé dish. Bake at 375° for 30 to 40 minutes. Serve immediately. Serves 4 to 6.

QUICHE ARGENTEUIL

8-INCH PASTRY CRUST   unbaked
FRESH ASPARAGUS   1 bunch
AUTUMN'S ASPARAGUS PURÉE (see index)   small amount
ONION   ¼ cup finely chopped
BUTTER or MARGARINE
HAM or VEAL   ¼ cup shredded
EGGS   2
HALF-AND-HALF   1 cup
PARMESAN CHEESE   6 ounces grated
GRUYÈRE CHEESE   6 ounces grated
HOLLANDAISE SAUCE (see index)

Make your favorite recipe for pastry or use a mix, and line pie pan with it. Cook half the well-trimmed asparagus until just crunchy-tender; drain. Cook the rest of the asparagus until thoroughly soft, and make a small recipe of Autumn's Asparagus Purée. Arrange tender spears in bottom of pie pan, immediately on top of pastry. Sauté onions until soft in butter. Sprinkle onions and ham over asparagus spears. Mix eggs, half-and-half, and cheeses and pour over all. Bake in 325° oven about 1 hour until set. While quiche bakes, mix asparagus purée and hollandaise sauce to desired consistency (approximately equal proportions) for sauce, and serve with quiche wedges. Serves 4 to 6 as entrée.

FIVE EASY SPARROWGRASS CRÊPES

Make your favorite crêpe batter or buy as many thin flour tortillas as you will need. Lightly butter the tortilla or crêpe and fill with the chosen filling; roll up or fold over and cover with appropriate sauce. Bake in a lightly greased baking dish at 350° for about 15 minutes. If using tortillas, take special care not to let them dry out—use sauce liberally, or bake on rack above a pan of water, or bake inside foil covering.

Each of the following filling recipes makes 1 serving:

No. 1

CHICKEN   ⅓ cup cooked and shredded
WATER CHESTNUTS   4, diced
AUTUMN'S ASPARAGUS PURÉE (see index)   1 tablespoon
SALT   to taste
GARLIC POWDER   to taste
MOZZARELLA CHEESE   slivers
AUTUMN'S ASPARAGUS PURÉE (see index)
HOLLANDAISE SAUCE (see index)

Combine chicken with water chestnuts and mound in center of crêpe. Top with purée and season with salt and garlic. Top all with cheese. Fold crêpe and cover with sauce made from equal proportions of purée and hollandaise sauce.

No. 2

ASPARAGUS SPEARS   6 small or 3 large (about 3 inches long)
CLAMANDAISE SAUCE (see index)
MONTEREY JACK CHEESE   grated

Cook asparagus until crunchy-tender and place in center of tortilla or crêpe. Top with ¹/₆ cup sauce; then cover all with cheese. Fold crêpe and cover with remaining sauce.

No. 3

PIQUANT PECAN SAUCE (see index)
CHICKEN   ⅓ cup cooked and shredded
PECAN PIECES   1 tablespoon
AUTUMN'S ASPARAGUS PURÉE (see index)
SALT   to taste

Make sauce ahead of time and allow to solidify in refrigerator overnight. Combine chicken with pecans and purée; add salt and fill crêpe. Fold crêpe and spread sauce on it before baking; or bake in foil without sauce and bring hot sauce to the table.

No. 4

ASPARAGUS SPEARS   3 small (about 3 inches long)
CHICKEN   ⅓ cup cooked and shredded
WATER CHESTNUTS   2, diced
CLAMANDAISE SAUCE (see index)   1 tablespoon
PECAN PIECES   1 tablespoon
BUTTER
MONTEREY JACK CHEESE   grated

Cook asparagus until crunchy-tender and place in middle of crêpe. Combine chicken and water chestnuts, and place on top of asparagus. Top with sauce and pecans. Fold crêpe, butter the outside, and cover generously with cheese.

No. 5

ASPARAGUS SPEARS   3 small (about 3 inches long)
HUMMUS   1 tablespoon*
BLACK OLIVES   chopped
HAM AND HUMMUS SAUCE (see index)
ONION   minced
LEMON JUICE

Cook asparagus until crunchy-tender and place in middle of crêpe. Soak onion in lemon juice. Combine hummus, olives, sauce, and onion. Fold crêpe and cover with sauce.

*Buy canned, or purée cooked garbanzo beans with olive oil, vinegar or lemon juice, salt, and spices in blender.

Dessert and Oddments

For a long time, I doubted there could be a really good asparagus dessert. I did not intend to have one in this book, even after I learned from James Beard that the Biltmore Coffee Shop in Pershing Square in Los Angeles once served asparagus with vanilla sauce. But when I tasted this simple but elegant dish created by Anne Baldwin of Portola Valley, California, I decided to include it.

EMERALD CRÈME

FRESH ASPARAGUS   12 spears
WATER   1 tablespoon
HEAVY CREAM   ½ cup
POWDERED SUGAR   1 tablespoon
RUM   1 tablespoon

Cook asparagus until tender but not discolored (color is important here). Cut into small pieces and purée in blender with water. If any stringiness appears, press purée through a sieve. Whip cream and stir into purée, adding sugar and rum. Chill. Serves 1.

SPARROWGRASS SAUCE

Mix Autumn's Asparagus Purée (see index) in equal parts with hollandaise sauce (see index or use the canned variety) as sauce for vegetables, especially cauliflower, zucchini, or scalloped potatoes. Delicious on omelettes, quiches, and crêpes, and can also be used for meats, fish, and shellfish.

These two recipes are from the world's oldest surviving cookbook, Apicius's Roman cookery book, compiled by the epicure M. Gavius Apicius. The story is told that when Apicius counted his fortune after several years of high living and found that he had spent 100 million sesterces (mainly on food) and had only 10 million sesterces left, he committed suicide. Apicius lived almost 2,000 years ago, and the surviving manuscript of his book dates from the third century A.D., with additions by a fourth- or fifth-century editor.

A *patina* is a broad, shallow pan or dish the Romans used for cooking and perhaps for serving; thus these two recipes translate as "asparagus skillet suppers."

COLD ASPARAGUS PATINA

Pound cleaned asparagus in a mortar. Add water, beat well, and pass through a sieve. Into a saucepan put fig-peckers (small birds) that are ready to cook. In the mortar pound 6 scruples of pepper, moistening with *liquamen* (a salty sauce made from fish and wine boiled down together) and with 1 cyathus each of wine and *passum* (a specially prepared cooking wine; modern substitute is a very sweet Spanish wine); put in a saucepan with 3 ounces of oil, and bring to a boil. In a greased shallow pan, mix 6 eggs with *oenogarum* (*liquamen* mixed with fresh wine), add the asparagus purée, pour on the pepper, wine, and sauce mixture, and arrange the birds over all. Cook in the hot ashes, let cool, sprinkle with pepper, and serve.

HOT ASPARAGUS PATINA

Pound asparagus tips in the mortar, add wine, and sieve. Pound pepper, lovage, fresh coriander, savory, and onion, moistened with wine, *liquamen,* and oil. After pouring purée and spices into a greased shallow pan, you may break eggs over it when it is on the fire, so that the mixture sets. Sprinkle with finely ground pepper and serve.

SPARROWGRASS TORTE

FRESH ASPARAGUS   1 pound or
    FROZEN ASPARAGUS   1 10-ounce package
BUTTER or MARGARINE
FRESH MUSHROOMS   ½ pound chopped coarsely
CONDENSED CREAM OF SHRIMP SOUP   1 10½-ounce can
PREPARED HORSERADISH   1 teaspoon
SOURDOUGH FRENCH BREAD CRUMBS   2 cups fine and dry
MILK   1 to 2 tablespoons
FLOUR   1½ tablespoons
EGGS   4, separated
SALT   ½ teaspoon
CREAM CHEESE   1 4-ounce package
CHIVES   1 teaspoon snipped

Cook asparagus and cut into 1-inch pieces; drain, add butter, and keep hot. Reserve cooking liquid. Combine mushrooms with soup, diluted to desired consistency with asparagus cooking liquid; add horseradish; cook together briefly and keep hot. Grease 3 cake pans and spread each with bread crumbs. For pancakes, add milk to flour to make thin paste; add egg yolks and salt and beat well. Beat whites stiff but not dry and combine with flour mixture. Divide batter into 3 pans and bake at 350° for 15 to 20 minutes or until set.* Place first pancake on serving dish and spread with asparagus. Put second pancake on top and spread with softened cream cheese mixed with chives. Lay third pancake on top and pour mushroom-shrimp sauce over it, letting it run down over all. Serve immediately. Serves 8.

*You can also make pancakes using your own recipe or a mix.

Index

140

OTHER PAPERBACKS FROM PACIFIC SEARCH PRESS

COOKING

Bone Appétit! Natural Foods for Pets by Frances Sheridan Goulart. Treat your pet to some home-cooked meals made only with pure, natural ingredients. Recipes fit for both man and beast! Drawings. 96 pp. $2.95.

The Carrot Cookbook by Ann Saling. Over 200 mouth-watering recipes. Drawings. 160 pp. $3.50.

The Crawfish Cookbook by Norma Upson. Try the lobster's freshwater cousin, the crayfish, for inexpensive gourmet dining. Over 100 recipes for every time of day. Drawings. 160 pp. $3.95.

The Dogfish Cookbook by Russ Mohney. Over 65 piscine delights. Cartoons and drawings. 108 pp. $1.95.

The Green Tomato Cookbook by Paula Simmons. More than 80 solutions to the bumper crop. 96 pp. $2.95.

Wild Mushroom Recipes by the Puget Sound Mycological Society. 2d edition. Over 200 recipes. 176 pp. $6.95.

The Zucchini Cookbook by Paula Simmons. Revised and enlarged 2d edition. Over 150 tasty creations. 160 pp. $3.50.

NATURE

Butterflies Afield in the Pacific Northwest by William Neill/Douglas Hepburn, photography. Lovely guide with 74 unusual color photos of living butterflies. 96 pp. $5.95.

Cascade Companion by Susan Schwartz/Bob and Ira Spring, photography. Nature and history of the Washington Cascades. Black-and-white photos, maps. 160 pp. $5.95.

Common Seaweeds of the Pacific Coast by J. Robert Waaland. Introduction to the world of the seaweed—its biology, conservation, and many uses to both industry and seafood lovers. 42 color photos, diagrams, illustrations. 128 pp. $5.95

Fire and Ice: The Cascade Volcanoes by Stephen L. Harris. Copublished with the Mountaineers. Black-and-white photos and drawings, maps. 320 pp. $7.95.

Little Mammals of the Pacific Northwest by Ellen Kritzman. The only book of its kind devoted solely to the Northwest's little mammals. 48 color and black-and-white photos, distribution maps, index. 128 pp. $5.95.

Living Shores of the Pacific Northwest by Lynwood Smith/Bernard Nist, photography. Fascinating guide to seashore life. Over 140 photos, 110 in color. 160 pp. $9.95.

Minnie Rose Lovgreen's Recipe for Raising Chickens by Minnie Rose Lovgreen. 2d edition. 32 pp. $2.00.

Sleek & Savage: North America's Weasel Family by Delphine Haley. Extraordinary color and black-and-white photos; bibliography. 128 pp. $5.50.

Why Wild Edibles? The Joys of Finding, Fixing, and Tasting—West of the Rockies by Russ Mohney. Color and black-and-white photos, illustrations. 320 pp. $6.95.